# FLAGS

# FLAGS

★

## KENT ALEXANDER

### DR. WHITNEY SMITH, CONSULTING EDITOR
#### THE FLAG RESEARCH CENTER
#### WINCHESTER, MASSACHUSETTS

MALLARD
PRESS

**A FRIEDMAN GROUP BOOK**

Published by MALLARD PRESS
An Imprint of BDD Promotional Book
Company, Inc.
666 Fifth Avenue
New York, N.Y. 10103

Mallard Press and the accompanying duck logo
are registered trademarks of BDD Promotional
Book Co., Inc. registered in the U.S. Patent and
Trademark Office.

ISBN 0-7924-5752-8

*FLAGS*
was prepared and produced by
Michael Friedman Publishing Group, Inc.
15 West 26th Street
New York, New York 10010

Editor: Elizabeth Viscott Sullivan
Art Director: Jeff Batzli
Designer: Robert Michaels
Photography Editors: Christopher C. Bain
                                    Grace How

All national and state flags © The Flag Research
Center, Winchester, Massachusetts

Typeset by Classic Type, Inc.
Color separations by
United South Sea Graphic Art Co.
Printed and bound in Hong Kong by
Leefung-Asco Printers Ltd.

The publisher, author, and consulting editor
wish to acknowledge that extensive efforts
have been made to insure that this book be as
accurate as possible at the time of printing.

## DEDICATION

This book is dedicated to the children
of the world who will, with time, find
independence, peace, and harmony.
May their future be filled with truth
and tolerance.

## ACKNOWLEDGMENTS

This book could not have been done
without the assistance of the librarians
of the Enoch Pratt Library in Baltimore,
Maryland; the kindness of Mrs. Esther
Jackson, a retired schoolteacher now
working at the Star Spangled Banner
House in Baltimore; the aid of Teresa
Buerkle; the help of my editor, Elizabeth
Sullivan; and the expertise of Dr. Whitney
Smith.

# *FOREWORD*

If we could be given a single piece of paper from the future, nothing would give more information in that amount of space than illustrations of the world's national flags. The rise of nations, the fall of empires, the influence of religion, new ideological trends—all would be apparent in this snapshot view.

Likewise, history is dramatically and clearly expressed in the flags of the past and present. Great historical points such as 1815, 1848, 1918, 1939, 1945, and 1991 are summed up in the changes in national flags and the symbolisms they contain. This book then is not merely entertainment (flags as the floral border of the garden of history), and it is not simply a reference source (the world in colorful rectangles). *FLAGS* is an important view of humankind's past, its struggles for change, its self-image, and its hopes for the future.

No one book can pretend to encompass the vast subject of flags: a century ago Admiral George Preble wrote a volume of 815 pages on American flags without exhausting his subject. This book does, however, give an excellent intro-duction to flags, review the national flags as they stand today, and take a look at other flags of importance. In doing so, *FLAGS* demon-strates the often unappreciated importance of the subject.

*FLAGS* is also an implicit invitation to you to join the world of vexillology, the study of flag his-tory and symbolism. (This word derives from *vexillum,* the Latin word for flag, and *-ology,* "the study of.") Many people enjoy flags as a hobby; they collect, design, make, record, trade, and dis-play flags. There are museums and exhibits of flags; magazines are published for vexillologists; associations and conferences provide flag-related activities worldwide. For more informa-tion, see the Resources section on page 167.

Enjoy this book—and flags. In doing so, you are participating in a drama that spans the entire planet, from your neighborhood school flag to the massed banners of political protest to the flag planted on the moon. Flags go back at least five thousand years, yet appear daily in newspapers and on television. Any interest in flags, serious or casual, will be richly rewarded.

**Dr. Whitney Smith**
**The Flag Research Center**
**Winchester, Massachusetts**

# TABLE of CONTENTS

# Introduction

The people's flag is deepest red;
It shrouded oft our martyred dead,
And ere their limbs grew stiff and cold,
Their heart's blood dyed its every fold.

Then raise the scarlet standard high!
Within its shade we'll live or die.
Tho' cowards flinch and traitors sneer,
We'll keep the red flag flying here.

James M. Connell, "The Red Flag"

It is indeed a powerful sight to watch a nation's flag stand against the wind, for its brilliant colors and unique design are an explicit expression of that country's people, land, government, and ideals. In fact, a flag is often the impetus to stir people to courage and sacrifice; some would readily die rather than see their national flag fall to dishonor and disgrace. A flag also can represent goals of peace or hostility; it can belong to a nation of conquerors or it can be a cherished symbol of a people rightfully struggling to be free. Some flags, such as the Red Cross and the United Nations flags, represent ideals of international organizations, while others represent regional groups, such as NATO and the Council of Europe. Some flags symbolize struggles, such as black liberation, and religions, such as Judaism, Islam, and Christianity. Even the Girl and Boy Scouts of America and the International Scouts fly their own flags. Since antiquity, wherever people have marched forward, they have carried some type of banner to serve as a rallying point, a symbol of their loyalty and allegiance to their country or cause.

Every nation possesses at least one flag that is an external expression of how that country sees itself. If a nation sees itself as a Moslem nation, for example, it might use the symbol of the crescent moon on its flag to show the world that its inhabitants are followers of Islam. Flown at formal and informal occasions by border guards and embassies, and at countless other official ceremonies worldwide, the flag asserts the existence and importance of a nation and/or state. The flag also is a concrete reminder of a country's patriots, hopes for a better future, the promise of its political systems and religions, and sacrifices of past generations. When a nation's flag is added to the lineup of existing flags that fly in front of the United Nations building in New York City, that nation has reached the symbolic equivalent of being recognized as a true independent entity, a free nation.

Yet, while flags are commonplace to us, most of us know very little about them. We can recognize several national flags, but as a rule, we know little about a flag's history and its symbolism. In fact, people of all ages are drawn to flags, but most have no idea why they are flown. However, the better we can understand flag symbolism, the better will be the systems of communication among ourselves and our global neighbors.

This book is an introduction to flags and their histories. The anatomy of a flag is examined here as well as the colors and symbols that adorn modern-day flags. Also included is a brief background on the art of European heraldry, to which many flags owe a great deal.

It is important to understand that while some flags have a very detailed history, such as the Union Flag of Great Britain, the Danish flag, or the Stars and Stripes of the United States, many countries did not keep written records of their flags' transitions through the years. Many African countries only obtained freedom in the 1960s, and their flags do not have the same type of history as do the flags of Western countries that dominated world history in earlier times. In fact, many countries do not carry on about their flag, but fly it with a quiet dignity.

Today, a national flag is considered to be the symbol of its country's people, despite the fact that variations exist regarding the way in which each country regulates its flag's uses. Some countries, such as the United States, have a great many rules about the proper care of their flags, which may be the reason why there are often problems regarding "proper usage" in these places. Other countries, such as Great Britain and Denmark, have no set rules that govern a citizen's behavior with regard to displaying their flags; for example, the British Union Flag often adorns umbrellas and clothing, and the Danish flag is often painted on the faces of young children. Also, in many countries, such as India, it is rare to find the national flag hoisted over a private home.

No matter what the rules regarding usage are, most people feel a strong allegiance to their country's flag. And while flags are not as revered today as they used to be, they still serve as symbols of unity and reveal a great deal about the political and philosophical differences between nations. This is why it is important to keep an open mind about how each country views its flag. In a sense, flags are visual diplomats that, if understood, can permit a better comprehension of other cultures—and our own. Perhaps a deeper understanding of the world's flags can help lead the way for a brighter— and more colorful—future.

## FLAG EVOLUTION

When most people picture a flag, most see a piece of fabric attached to a rope, staff, or pole. But long before modern flags were invented, early civilizations carried wooden staffs whose tops bore carved symbols of earthly rulers or gods. These early flags were used in the same way we use flags today—to signal or to demonstrate loyalty.

The first evidence we have of flags comes from ancient Egypt. The Egyptians used these early "flags" to identify various parts of the empire. They also connected streamers to the tops of tall lances and poles and carried them into battle, perhaps in the belief that the flags would win them favor with the gods and, consequently, result in victory. The Assyrians and, later, the ancient Greeks and Romans used streamers in a similar fashion as well as to identify troops at a distance.

Most likely it was in battle that flags first gained importance. Generals saw their flags from afar and used them to locate their legions. Archers watched the direction in which the enemy flag's fabric blew, and knew to aim their arrows in the same direction, making arrow flight easier and more accurate.

*Military flags inspire, threaten, honor, and lead soldiers into battle.*

Many of the symbols used on flags date back thousands of years. The crescent moon appears on many Islamic nations' flags, just as the cross appears on the flags of many Christian countries. The Shield of David, commonly referred to as "the Star of David," is an ancient Jewish symbol and appears on the flag of Israel. The five-pointed star has often been used as a symbol during the past two hundred years; it usually represents statehood, unity, or sovereignty.

Other ancient civilizations of the Middle East, as well as Greece and Rome, employed symbols in similar fashions. There is evidence from the art of the ancient Greeks that they bore on their circular battle shields a wide variety of figures such as dogs, boars, horses, lions, birds, fish, and various other objects. In 500 B.C., Aeschylus recorded that these emblems adorned the shields of the attackers of Thebes. Rome's legions had their insignia, too: Virgil speaks of *insignia paternum* (loosely translated, "insignia of the father") on the shield of Aventinus.

The Romans not only made the most use of these symbols but also introduced the first true flag into the Western world, the vexillum, which, unlike most modern flags, was always attached to a horizontal pole. There is also evidence that the Teutonic peoples used flaglike devices, although these were probably tribal identifications rather than personal ones. The famous Bayeux tapestry (an eleventh-century tapestry over two hundred feet [60 m] long and one and two-thirds feet [50 cm] wide) depicts the incidents leading up to the Norman conquest in A.D. 1066, and is a fine example of a cloth visual history, with its record of Norman and Saxon shields and banners decorated with the figures of birds, beasts, crosses, and other arcane forms.

Although it is difficult to date the following developments, it is reported that flags attached along one side to an upright pole first appeared in ancient China and were introduced to Western civilization by the Arabs; at the time, flags were usually made of linen. Also, ancient Moslem armies carried flags bearing Islamic inscriptions; early Christians marched under the symbol of the cross; and halfway around the world, in Mexico, the Aztecs made flags of feathers, which their warriors wore on their backs as they rode into battle.

The practice of using flags in times of war, both to recognize troops and to inspire young men to fight more fiercely in the defense of a cause, was vigorously instigated in the West with the great Crusades, military expeditions undertaken in the eleventh, twelfth, and thirteenth centuries to win the Holy Land from the Moslems. For it was then, for the first time in history, that thousands of people from different Christian countries formed a single army and marched across Europe and Asia Minor to forcibly spread Christianity.

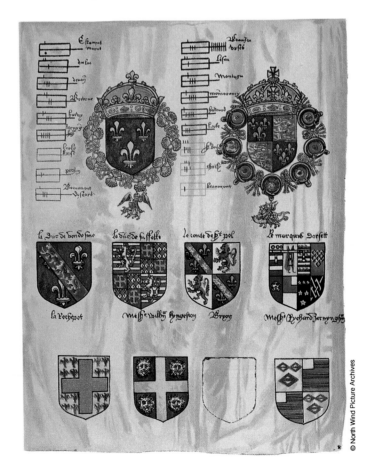

*Heraldry established many of the rules for good flag design and usage; it also created striking symbols.*

At the time, the soldiers often wore armor that fully covered their bodies and most of their faces. Consequently, it was imperative that each person have a way to find his lord and commander quickly and easily in battle. Such identification was probably realized by the carrying of lance pennons and banners in distinctive colors. The hardship of carrying such markers was soon overcome by the creation of colored surcoats, padded garments made of linen that were worn over the armor to protect it from the elements. The soldiers also chose personal emblems to adorn their surcoats and shields. These were often an animal or bird whose courage they wanted to imitate. Often, too, these emblems were variations of the Christian cross, which they had pledged to wear while embarking on the holy wars.

Before long, the surcoats and banners were of the same design and, because there were soon hundreds of designs, symbols had to be chosen with care in order not to infringe upon another's. Organically then, a system of regulation was created to monitor, devise, assign, and record insignia. Thus, the art and science of heraldry, born sometime in the 1200s, came into existence simultaneously in several Western European countries and reached its fruition in the Middle Ages.

The herald's job was, in part, to identify and record these insignia, or coats of arms, and to create and assign new ones. In the broadest sense, the herald (taken from the German *des heares zu walten,* which means "manager of the troops") was responsible for proclaiming and conducting jousting tournaments; transporting messages between kings, princes, and armies; and for overseeing royal ceremonies. Because he performed these functions, the herald had to recognize men by their shields and pennons, so he inadvertently became a genealogist who traced and recorded family history through his knowledge of symbols, which were often passed down from father to son or son-in-law.

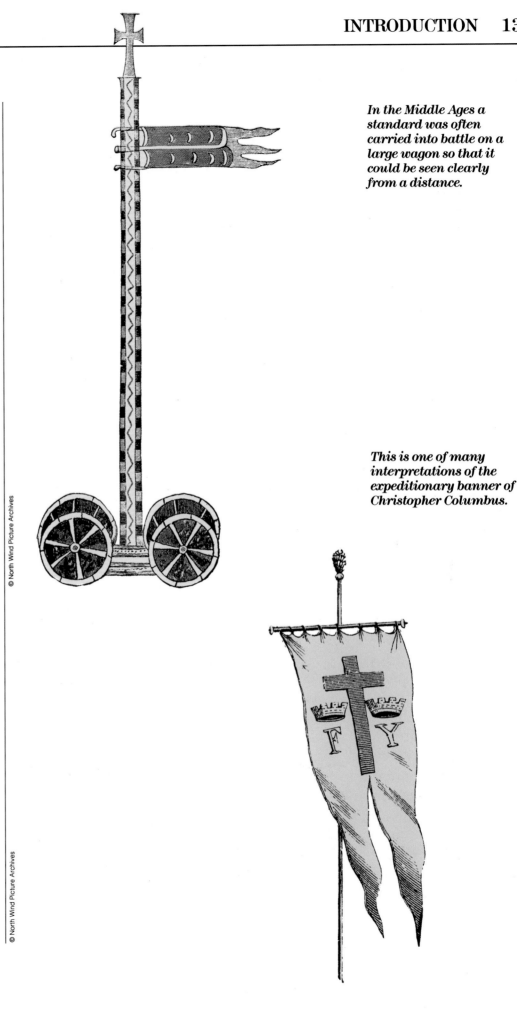

*In the Middle Ages a standard was often carried into battle on a large wagon so that it could be seen clearly from a distance.*

*This is one of many interpretations of the expeditionary banner of Christopher Columbus.*

© North Wind Picture Archives

© North Wind Picture Archives

The art of heraldry produced three early types of flags: the pennon, the banner, and the standard. The pennon is a small flag, either pointed or swallow-tailed at the fly and borne immediately below the lance head. This ensign, or flag, was used by a knight or a regiment of lancers. The banner is usually square or oblong, with its depth being greater than its breadth. This flag was carried at the end of a lance or spear; it was the flag of the military chief and used as the rallying point for troops. The standard is a narrow and tapering flag. It has always been of considerable length—its length is in direct relationship to the rank of its owner.

As the Middle Ages ended, heraldry's importance waned, and it became a primarily symbolic and decorative art. Although traditional heraldic symbols such as the rampant lion and spread eagle can still be seen on flags as well as on official seals for many European countries such as Germany, Finland, and Sweden, they are seldom relied upon to denote identity. Nevertheless, most experts agree that this early form of symbol classification was the predecessor of today's flag design.

## JAPANESE HERALDRY

The only other system in the world that rivals European heraldry is the Japanese one of stylized emblems called *mon*. These emblems are simplified, symmetrical versions of everyday objects, such as cherry blossoms, hollyhocks, or chrysanthemums. In fact, the imperial flag of modern Japan contains a *mon* depicting a stylized chrysanthemum. Until very recently, all Japanese flags were a part of this system in which, like European heraldic symbols, the *mon* badges were used as hereditary family badges. It has only been in the twentieth century that *mon* have come to be used to symbolize places such as cities, provinces, or Japan itself.

The rising sun has been a Japanese emblem for thousands of years; the chrysanthemum is a personal symbol of the emperor.

## THE EMERGENCE OF THE MODERN FLAG

Of course, under the feudal system there was no concept of nationality as we have come to understand it. Kings, queens, and sometimes princes ruled territories and, in order to defend these kingdoms, they divided them up into fiefs, which they then distributed to barons in exchange for military support and other services. The barons, in turn, subdivided their land among lesser lords and knights. When the combined armies went to war, it was imperative that they fight under a common banner, and often that symbol was that of a patron saint. Several of these ancient symbols survive to this day; England's St. George's cross is a good example. But while some early nation's flags came into being in this manner, many developed through another route—the sea.

During the Middle Ages, when a ship carried cargo from port to port, it would fly the pennon of its owner from its masthead. Most often, a shipowner was a merchant and not of noble birth, so he was obliged to fly the flag of his home port, which was controlled and protected by a noble family or the church. This flag was a symbol of permission that granted the ship port entrance and afforded protection on the high seas. The merchant would simply pay a registration fee for the flag, then be free to sail and anchor at a port.

Because the flag had to be visible over great distances, often miles, a complicated banner would be ineffective, as it would not be quickly and clearly distinguished. Therefore, two stripes of fabric in the principal colors from the protector's coat of arms would often be sewn together to make a vertically or horizontally striped flag that could be easily recognized from afar. This need for long-distance recognition is why so

*Crusaders used both royal banners of heraldic design and simple flags with crosses to distinguish between the participating European nations.*

many of today's nations, including those with no sea borders, utilize national flags made from several colored stripes of fabric.

With the beginning of the Renaissance, European societies grew in size and slowly changed. Often, fortresses were no longer the property of the individual but of the state. As colonial empires began to flourish, competition grew between sovereign states. Ships of exploration and commerce traveled to all parts of the world and needed to have flags for identification. All of these trends (and others) resulted in the development of flags representing state power. Frequently the flags had coats of arms or other royal symbols to indicate the power of the ruling dynasty. Sometimes the colors only from coats of arms were used for stripes and, outside Europe, symbols from nature (the peacock of Burma, the sun of Japan, or the lion of Ethiopia, for example) appeared on flags. The cross in different variations was frequently used by Christian countries.

However, until the beginning of the 1800s, flags were viewed as symbols of a state's authority. A flag neither belonged to the people, nor represented them in any way. During the nineteenth century, many countries worldwide experienced a great deal of political upheaval. As new national consciousnesses and revolutionary attitudes emerged, workers, students, unionists, and political movements created flags to represent their struggles and aims. These flags, in turn, served as rallying points against their oppressors. If a cause was successful in overthrowing the powers of the state, its flag then became the new national symbol, representing the victory of the common man and woman; this was the case with the French Tricolor, as well as with the red banner of the Soviet Union. Almost every flag in North America, South America, and the independent nations of Africa was developed from revolutionary liberation struggle symbols.

## The Anatomy of a Flag

Flags come in different shapes and sizes. Today, most flags are made from polyester or nylon, although many different types of fabrics have been used in the past, such as cotton, linen, silk, and wool. Designs are created by sewing together fabric of different colors or are printed onto the flag's surface.

Since the 1600s, the majority of the flags used at sea have been rectangular; this same shape is considered standard for land-based flags. Military flags are by tradition square, while heraldic banners are usually squarish.

Flags are generally suspended from a vertical pole, although they can also be hung horizontally. Usually flown from a flagpole, a ship's halyard, or carried on spears, flags can also be affixed to metal or wooden pins to adorn tabletops. They are also hung at a forty-five-degree angle from a stout pole, known as a gaff, on a ship.

Flags are divided into four quarters, or cantons. The two quarters closest to the pole are the "hoist," and the remaining two are the fly quarters. The upper canton of the hoist, which often contains a badge or emblem, is often simply referred to as the canton. Flags flown from a pole have a tube of fabric called a heading, or a sleeve, on the hoist side. While most of the world's flags usually have a hoist rope sewn into the heading, flags of the United States normally have an eyelet at either end.

For either parade or indoor usage, the flagstaff is passed through the sleeve,

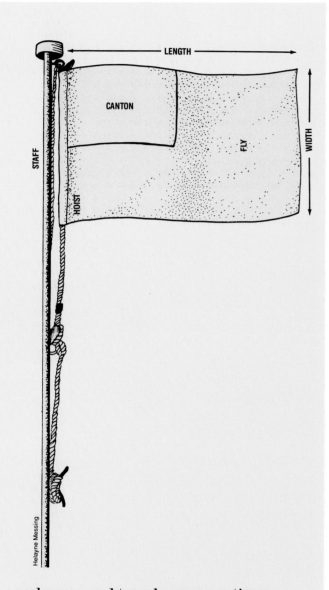

LENGTH

CANTON

FLY

STAFF

HOIST

WIDTH

Hellayne Messing

and ropes and tassels are sometimes attached below the finial (a small ornament at the end of a staff or pole). The horizontal dimension is the length of the flag, while the vertical dimension is its width. When showing the proportions of a flag, two numbers are used. The first number refers to the flag's width, and the second number pertains to its length. Therefore, a flag two (2) feet (30 cm) wide and four (4) feet (1.2 m) long is in proportions of 1:2.

## Colors and Their Meanings

There is no doubt that color truly elicits a relationship between the mental and the emotional; it stimulates us as well as satisfies something very deep in our hearts. People often refer to their flag as their "colors," and flags have depended on the use of color since antiquity. In battle, the ancient Greeks tied a purple cloth to the end of a spear to signal that a charge was about to commence. Signal flags, with their color-coded alphabet, were once used by navies to communicate at sea.

The following is a generalized color chart to help illustrate what each color means when used on a flag. Bear in mind that different countries often reinterpret colors (as well as other symbols) to coincide with their own political situations and beliefs.

**Yellow:** Yellow, a primary color, symbolizes the sun, illumination, and intelligence. Because it is close in color to the color gold, yellow symbolizes wealth or a golden future. The international symbol of a quarantine area is the yellow flag.

**Orange:** Orange is a secondary color, as it is a transition between yellow and red. Orange is used infrequently in flags. It may symbolize Hinduism, savannahs, or Protestantism. In early Dutch flags, it honored Prince William of Orange.

**Red:** Red is a powerful primary color. Because of its intensity, red demands our immediate attention. Red also stirs our emotions and, by doing so, compels action. Because it seems to advance toward the eye, red has been the basic symbol of fire since ancient times. It also suggests aggressive vibration and movement. It symbolizes the spiritual fires of purification, divine passion, consuming love, and sovereign power. Red also can represent dynamic health, or "red-blooded" individuals or people.

Red can also symbolize war, rage, and hatred. Often red stands for the spilling of blood and represents such in early United States flags and present-day Latin American and African flags. A simple red flag is used to signal "Stop!" and to warn of danger and explosives.

**Purple:** Purple is a secondary color and is the transitional color between red and blue. Purple is used to denote imperial power, dignity, wealth, and royalty.

**Blue:** Blue, a primary color, has the opposite effect of red: It does not demand our attention and it does not stimulate action. Blue is often used to symbolize water and the sky. Christian flags sometimes use blue to symbolize devotion to Mary, the mother of Christ.

**Green:** Green is a secondary color, the transitional color between yellow and blue. As the color of spring, green symbolizes growth, renewal, and hope. Because it is also the color of trees and plants, green represents nature. It is a refreshing color, symbolizing life over death.

**White:** White is the combination of all colors and is the ultimate in terms of symbols of brightness and lightness. White is used to symbolize purity, innocence, revelation, and peace. A white flag means surrender or truce.

**Black:** Although it sometimes appears in their national heraldry, black symbolizes death and mourning to many Europeans. To Africans and other dark people of the world, however, black is a symbol of pride, unity, and victory over oppression. In Arab flags, it recalls the black banners supposedly used by Muhammad.

**The Rainbow:** The rainbow is rarely used as a flag symbol. However, when it appears on a flag, it usually represents peace, gay rights, or environmental concern.

# *HOW TO USE THIS BOOK*

There are hundreds of national flags, each of which has grown out of a specific set of objective conditions. Many of these circumstances are, of course, interrelated. For example, a new flag often contains elements of an older flag and might bear the colors or the emblem of the principal colonializer of the region. Upon gaining independence, an emerging nation will often pattern its flag after the colors and symbols of another country, a local political organization, or dominant religion that embodies its ideals. Such patterning is evident in color choice, seen on those flags that are modeled after the French Tricolor, or in symbol choice, such as the star and crescent moon.

In this book, the flags are ordered geographically. Each chapter is devoted to one of the seven continents and thus will cover each country in that continent by plotting a course from north to south, or east to west; the continent of Africa is an exception to this rule. Finally, chapter nine takes a look at flags that are internationally recognized.

In chapter one, Africa, the course will differ from the rest of the book, since Africa has so many countries and possesses several different groups of flags; and more importantly, many of its emerging nations derive their flags from their dominant political party. The African unity flags (those flags that share colors that have been designated by their users as being symbolic of the African liberation movement) will be grouped together, as will the families of flags that share the symbols of Islam or Arab unity. Also linked will be those countries that have a conscious desire to have no overt political statement represented by their national colors.

In *Flags*, every entry concentrates on a particular country and the developments that gave birth to that country's national flag. The conditions that created each flag are identified, as is any relationship that the flag might have to other flags within or outside of its flag family.

## *FLAG FAMILIES*

A flag family is a group of flags that share common design elements or a common background. For example, the flags belonging to the family of flags that represent communist ideals often display the five-pointed gold star of communism. Also, many African and Arab countries share common flag colors as well as the symbols that express their goals of African or Arab unity. The following are several important flag families that should be helpful in using this book:

**Pan-African:** The colors of the pan-African flags originate from two different sources. The black-red-green flags can be traced back to Jamaican-born Marcus Garvey, who in the 1930s organized and headed the Universal Negro Improvement Association, the largest organization to date of

African-Americans. This flag was combined in the West Indies during the 1930s with the green-yellow-red of Ethiopia, and both flags bear colors representing toil, revolutionary struggle, and unity. This combination also gave rise to the Rastafarian colors and to the flag of Ghana and its many offspring—all flags whose countries allied themselves with African identity and liberation. These colors are also often found in use in the Caribbean as well as in African-American liberation movement flags in the United States.

**Pan-Arab:** These colors were first used before the beginning of World War I. However, after the Arab revolt of 1917, in which the former Arab lands of the Turkish empire gained independence, the colors came to be used widely in national flags. Originally, the four colors were used only by the Hashemite states set up in those territories, but today they are widely used throughout countries wishing to proclaim their common Arab ties. This flag family also includes

a later generation of flags (red, white, and black), which were first used by Egypt in its 1952 revolution.

**Pan-Slavic:** These flags are all variations of the Imperial Russian flag and include not only the flag of Bulgaria, but also the current flag of Czechoslovakia.

**Tricolors:** These flags originated in vertical tricolor combinations that emerged during the French Revolution and emulated its ideals.

**The Red Flag:** These flags are based on the Red Flag used during the French Revolution. Since that time the Red Flag has been used by many countries with communist governments.

**Flags of Islam:** These flags were inspired by the crescent and star flag of Turkey. Flags of this family can be found from Morocco to Malaysia, and many of them also display the color green, believed to have been the favorite color of the prophet Muhammad.

*ETHIOPIA; PAN-AFRICAN*

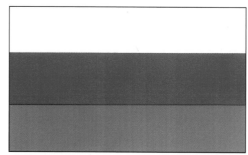

*BULGARIA; PAN-SLAVIC*

*CHINA; RED FLAG*

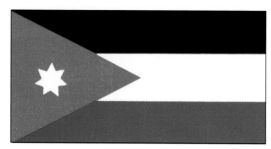

*JORDAN; PAN-ARAB*

*FRANCE; TRICOLOR*

*TURKEY; FLAG OF ISLAM*

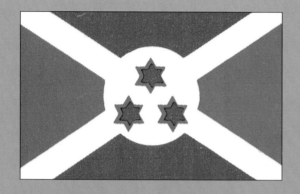  

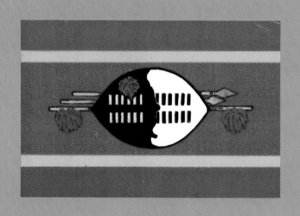  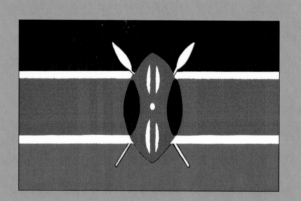

# CHAPTER ONE

# *Africa*

Most flags of the African continent have emerged from a history of struggle for freedom from years of European colonial bondage. Many African nations obtained their hard-fought independence through revolutionary struggle and the work of lawyers and politicians such as Kwame Nkrumah and Jomo Kenyatta, the respective fathers of Ghana and Kenya. When the people of the new African nations began the task of designing their flags, they turned their eyes toward Ethiopia, a country that, until the invasion of Italian troops in 1936, had remained free of colonization. Ethiopia was admired for its resistance to the Italians, and the green, yellow, and red colors of its flag were adopted first by the nation of Ghana, and later, by many other countries that wanted the world to recognize that not only were they independent African nations, but that they yearned for an Africa controlled by Africans as well.

See page 19 for more information on the pan-African colors.

# EGYPT

Egypt, after a 1919 revolt against England, became an independent nation in 1922. The first distinctive Egyptian flag was green with a white crescent and three stars. The Arab Liberation Flag of 1952 had red-white-black stripes and a central gold eagle. The green flag was replaced by the Arab Liberation Flag in 1958 when Egypt and Syria founded the United Arab Republic. At that time, two green stars were substituted for seals. Egypt flew this flag until 1972, when, with Libya and Syria, it founded the Federation of Arab Republics. Egypt maintained the tricolor flag, but opted to use the emblem of the golden hawk (taken from Syria's arms) instead of the two stars. In 1984, Egypt replaced the golden hawk with the Eagle of Saladin, the original badge of the Arab Socialist Union that became the arms of the UAR in 1958.

*Since ancient times, travelers to Egypt have visited the Sphinx.*

© Steve Vidler/Leo de Wys, Inc.

| EGYPT | |
|---|---|
| Official Name: | Arab Republic of Egypt |
| Capital: | Cairo |
| Languages: | Arabic |
| Religions: | Muslim, Coptic Christian, others |
| Exports: | Petroleum, cotton, cotton yarn, fabric |
| Imports: | Food, machinery, fertilizer, transportation equipment |
| Highest Point: | 8,668 ft. (2,642 m) |
| Lowest Point: | -436 ft. (-133 m) |
| Area: | 386,643 sq. mi. (1,001,019 sq km) |

# SUDAN

The Sudan won independence from Britain in 1956 and, until 1970, flew a tricolor of blue, yellow, and green. These colors were said to symbolize respectively the Nile, the desert, and the country's fertile regions. In 1970, as a result of a design competition, the present flag was approved. The colors were derived from the Arab Liberation Flag, although coincidentally they were already in use by the nationalist Umma party of the Sudan in a different configuration. The colors are now interpreted as follows: red represents revolution; white, peace; green, fertility; and black, the destruction of colonialism.

| SUDAN | |
|---|---|
| Official Name: | Republic of the Sudan |
| Capital: | Khartoum |
| Languages: | Arabic, indigenous, English |
| Religions: | Sunni Muslim, indigenous, Christian |
| Exports: | Cotton, gum arabic, peanuts, sesame |
| Imports: | Petroleum products, machinery, textiles |
| Highest Point: | 10,456 ft. (3,187 m) |
| Lowest Point: | Sea level |
| Area: | 967,500 sq. mi. (2,504,857 sq km) |

# MALAWI

Malawi gained its independence from Britain in 1964. The colors in its national flag are not only the red, black, and green of the United Negro Improvement Association begun by Marcus Garvey, but of the Malawi Congress party, under which Malawi won independence. At independence, the symbolism of the flag's colors was altered, and the stylized sun image was added. The black is said to represent Africa; the red, the blood shed in the struggle for freedom; and the green, Malawi's fields and forests. The sun represents the dawn (or *kwacha*, also the name of Malawi's currency) and the hope of freedom for all Africa.

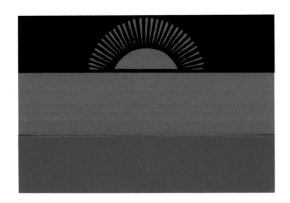

| MALAWI | |
|---|---|
| Official Name: | Republic of Malawi |
| Capital: | Lilongwe |
| Languages: | Tombuka |
| Religions: | Protestant, Roman Catholic, Muslim |
| Exports: | Tobacco, tea, sugar, peanuts |
| Imports: | Manufactured goods, machinery, fuels, motor vehicles |
| Highest Point: | 9,849 ft. (3,002 m) |
| Lowest Point: | 120 ft. (37 m) |
| Area: | 45,747 sq. mi. (118,439 sq km) |

# KENYA

Kenya became a republic in 1964 after gaining its independence from Britain in 1963. Kenya's national flag, inspired by the Garvey colors (see **Malawi**) was based on the flag of the Kenya African National Unity party (KANU) first adopted in 1951. The party flag had three stripes (green, red, black) with a shield and crossed assegais (spears) in a white center. The national flag is based directly on the party flag; however, the shield has a more elaborate form, and the red stripe has white fimbriations, added to represent the other dominant party, the Kenya African Democratic Union, which has since merged with KANU.

Jomo Kenyatta, leader of the independence movement, watched the flag hoisted officially when his country gained its freedom in 1963. He had first interpreted the symbolism of the flag eleven years earlier as follows:

> Black is to show that this is for the black people. Red is to show that the blood of an African is the same color as the blood of a European, and green is to show that when we were given this country by God it was green, fertile and good. [The shield and spear] mean that we should remember our forefathers who used these weapons to guard this land....

*BELOW: A Kenyan exhibits national pride at the 1988 Olympic Games in Seoul, South Korea.*

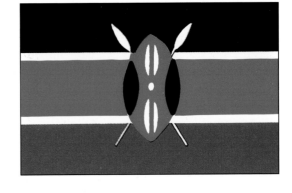

| KENYA | |
|---|---|
| Official Name: | Republic of Kenya |
| Capital: | Nairobi |
| Languages: | English, Swahili, indigenous |
| Religions: | Protestant, Catholic, indigenous |
| Exports: | Petroleum products, tea, coffee, livestock |
| Imports: | Petroleum, machinery, iron, steel |
| Highest Point: | 17,058 ft. (5,199 m) |
| Lowest Point: | Sea level |
| Area: | 224,961 sq. mi. (582,424 sq km) |

*ABOVE: Today both the wildlife of Africa and its natural habitat are endangered.*

# ETHIOPIA

Ethiopia, once called Abyssinia, has been a kingdom since at least A.D. 200, when immigrants from Saba in South Arabia helped set up the Aksum kingdom. Ethiopia is the oldest independent state in Africa, and its flag came into use in the 1890s, when its ancient monarchy was invaded by Italy. This flag, associated with the Coptic church, which was widely embraced in A.D. 330, inspired the Rastafarians, who believe that Haile Selassie, the former Ethiopian emperor, is divine. As emperor, Selassie's title was Conquering Lion of Judah; the lion, crowned and carrying a cross, appeared on the state flag.

The three bands of color are thought to have originally represented the three divisions of the Ethiopian army. These colors soon came to symbolize African unity: Green represents the country's forests and agriculture; yellow, its sunshine and precious gold; and red, the blood sacrificed by those warriors who defended the country against the Italians.

After Selassie was overthrown in 1974, the lion on the flag was stripped of its crown and cross, which were replaced with a spear. A new socialist emblem was added in 1984, but was revised in the constitution of 1987.

| ETHIOPIA | |
|---|---|
| Official Name: | Ethiopia |
| Capital: | Addis Ababa |
| Languages: | Amharic, Arabic, indigenous |
| Religions: | Muslim, Coptic Christian, animistic |
| Exports: | Coffee, hides and skins |
| Imports: | Petroleum, machinery, motor vehicles |
| Highest Point: | 15,158 ft. (4,620 m) |
| Lowest Point: | -381 ft. (-116 m) |
| Area: | 472,434 sq. mi. (1,223,131 sq km) |

# GHANA

Ghana, which became independent from Britain in 1957, was the third independent African nation (Liberia was the first, in 1847) and the first country to combine the original Ethiopian colors with the black of Marcus Garvey (see **pan-African** colors, page 19) in the form of a star emblem, also used by Garvey as a symbol of African unity. The flag was created by the father of Ghana, Kwame Nkrumah, but did not exactly reproduce the colors of his own political party. The color red is said to stand for those who fought the British for Ghana's freedom; the yellow, the natural resources of the nation and its colonial name, the "Gold Coast"; and the green, the agriculture and the forests of the country.

In 1964, in order to reflect the colors of Nkrumah's party, the yellow in the flag was altered to white; however, after a 1966 military coup in which Nkrumah fell from power, the flag returned to its former colors, which inspired many other pan-African flags.

| GHANA | |
|---|---|
| Official Name: | Republic of Ghana |
| Capital: | Accra |
| Languages: | English, Akan, indigenous |
| Religions: | Christian, indigenous, Muslim |
| Exports: | Cocoa, wood, gold |
| Imports: | Manufactured goods, fuels, food, transportation equipment |
| Highest Point: | 2,905 ft. (885 m) |
| Lowest Point: | Sea level |
| Area: | 92,100 sq. mi. (238,447 sq km) |

*The bright colors of Ashanti kings are found today in the flag of Ghana.*

*A small village in Senegal.*

# GUINEA

Guinea became independent from France in 1958. The colors of its flag intentionally replicate those of Ghana, for at one time both Kwame Nkrumah (see **Ghana**) and Sekou Toure, Guinea's first independence leader, wished to unite their two countries. It is reported that the Guinea Democratic party (a part of the Rassemblement Démocratique Africain, a political party that used the Ethiopian colors and fought for independence in the West African lands colonized by France) quickly decided to adopt the pan-African colors based on the design of the French Tricolor. (It is common, by the way, for former French colonies to pattern their flag after the Tricolor of France.)

| GUINEA | |
|---|---|
| Official Name: | People's Revolutionary Republic of Guinea |
| Capital: | Conakry |
| Languages: | French, indigenous |
| Religions: | Muslim, indigenous, Christian |
| Exports: | Bauxite, alumina, pineapples, coffee |
| Imports: | Petroleum, metals, machinery, transportation equipment |
| Highest Point: | 5,748 ft. (1,752 m) |
| Lowest Point: | Sea level |
| Area: | 94,926 sq. mi. (245,763 sq km) |

*A human figure (shown here on ceremonial headdress) formerly appeared on the flag of Mali.*

# MALI

The Federation of Mali was formed in 1959, and it was through the Federation that Mali became united with Senegal. At that time, Mali adopted a flag like its present one, modeled after the French Tricolor, but bearing the black outline of a human figure, a *kanaga*, in its center. The *kanaga* symbolized African consciousness; the Ethiopian colors represented the concept of unity with other African nations. In June 1960, the federation became independent and, in August of that same year, Mali and Senegal separated. Mali kept its name and the flag, but dropped the *kanaga* in March 1961.

| MALI | |
|---|---|
| Official Name: | Republic of Mali |
| Capital: | Bamako |
| Languages: | French, Bambara, indigenous |
| Religions: | Muslim, indigenous, Christian |
| Exports: | Cotton, livestock, dried fish, peanuts |
| Imports: | Food, machinery, vehicles, petroleum |
| Highest Point: | 3,789 ft. (1,155 m) |
| Lowest Point: | 300 ft. (91 m) |
| Area: | 478,766 sq. mi. (1,239,525 sq km) |

# SENEGAL

Senegal was once united with Mali and, consequently, shared that country's flag history (see **Mali**) until it seceded from the Mali Federation in August 1960. Once an independent nation, Senegal replaced the *kanaga* from the federation's flag with a green star. It is believed that the green star symbolizes independence. In 1982, Senegal formed a confederation with Gambia, known as Senegambia, but neither country's national symbols were affected by this allegiance, which ended in 1989.

| SENEGAL | |
|---|---|
| Official Name: | Republic of Senegal |
| Capital: | Dakar |
| Languages: | French, Wolof, indigenous |
| Religions: | Muslim, indigenous, Christian |
| Exports: | Peanuts and peanut products, phosphate rock, fish |
| Imports: | Food, consumer goods, machinery, petroleum |
| Highest Point: | 1,906 ft. (581 m) |
| Lowest Point: | Sea level |
| Area: | 75,955 sq. mi. (196,647 sq km) |

# CAMEROON

Cameroon adopted the pan-African colors in 1957, making it the second country (after Ghana) to do so. An autonomous French trusteeship until 1960, Cameroon did not then include the part of the British territory that later federated with it to form the present-day country. Like many other former French colonies, upon independence, Cameroon modeled its flag after the French Tricolor. The original flag carried no emblem, but in 1961, when the southern part of the region was linked with the federal state, two yellow stars were added to the green stripe to symbolize the union. In 1975, one star was removed, and the remaining star was moved to the center to represent a unified nation. The green at the hoist represents the vegetation of Cameroon's southern region and the hope of a prosperous future; red, the power joining the two halves of the federation; and yellow represents the sun as well as the wealth of the northern region.

| CAMEROON | |
|---|---|
| Official Name: | Republic of Cameroon |
| Capital: | Yaoundé |
| Languages: | English, French, indigenous |
| Religions: | Animistic, Christian, Muslim |
| Exports: | Petroleum, cocoa, coffee, wood |
| Imports: | Machinery, transportation equipment, petroleum products |
| Highest Point: | 13,451 ft. (4,100 m) |
| Lowest Point: | Sea level |
| Area: | 183,569 sq. mi. (475,260 sq km) |

# RWANDA

Rwanda, previously incorporated into German East Africa, was occupied by Belgium for more than forty years, until January 1961, when the dominant Hutu party declared Rwanda a republic. At that time, a flag resembling Guinea's was adopted. In September 1961, Rwanda added a large black letter 'R' to the center. When Rwanda became independent in 1962, this version of the flag was retained. The red of Rwanda's flag symbolizes the suffering of its people during the liberation struggle; yellow, the victory of the people's revolution; and green, hope. The letter 'R,' for which there is no official size or shape, stands for Rwanda, republic, and revolution.

| RWANDA | |
|---|---|
| Official Name: | Rwandan Republic |
| Capital: | Kigali |
| Languages: | Kinyarwanda, French |
| Religions: | Roman Catholic, indigenous, Protestant, Muslim |
| Exports: | Coffee, tea, cassiterite, wolfram |
| Imports: | Food, clothing, machinery, transportation equipment |
| Highest Point: | 14,787 ft. (4,507 m) |
| Lowest Point: | 1,200 ft. (366 m) |
| Area: | 10,169 sq. mi. (26,328 sq km) |

# GUINEA-BISSAU

Guinea-Bissau and the Cape Verde Islands were both colonized by the Portuguese and shared the same liberation movement, the Partido Africano da Independencia da Guiné e Cabo Verde (PAIGC). PAIGC's flag was similar to the present flag of Guinea-Bissau except that the party's initials were underneath the black star that symbolizes African unity. In 1973, PAIGC raised the current flag without the initials and declared Guinea-Bissau an independent country. One year later, Portugal recognized the nation's status.

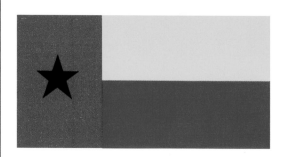

| GUINEA-BISSAU | |
|---|---|
| Official Name: | Republic of Guinea-Bissau |
| Capital: | Bissau |
| Languages: | Portuguese, indigenous |
| Religions: | Indigenous, Muslim, Christian |
| Exports: | Peanuts, palm kernels, shrimp |
| Imports: | Food, machinery, transportation equipment, fuels |
| Highest Point: | 1,017 ft. (310 m) |
| Lowest Point: | Sea level |
| Area: | 13,948 sq. mi. (36,111 sq km) |

# CAPE VERDE

Cape Verde's flag is similar to the flag of Guinea-Bissau (see **Guinea-Bissau**). However, the flag's proportions are different, and its black star (representing African unity) has a wreath of maize (symbolizing the people's food) with a clamshell centered underneath it. Originally, the clamshell symbolized the islands, but it now represents Cape Verde's fishing industry. Cape Verde used the PAIGC flag until it became an independent country in 1975.

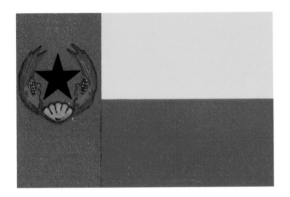

| CAPE VERDE | |
|---|---|
| Official Name: | Republic of Cape Verde |
| Capital: | Praia |
| Languages: | Portuguese, Crioulo |
| Religions: | Roman Catholic |
| Exports: | Fish, bananas, salt |
| Imports: | Petroleum products, corn, rice, machinery |
| Highest Point: | 9,281 ft. (2,829 m) |
| Lowest Point: | Sea level |
| Area: | 1,557 sq. mi. (4,031 sq km) |

# TOGO

Togo, when under trusteeship of France, used a flag of green with two yellow stars with the French Tricolor in its canton. In 1960, when Togo gained independence, it diverted from the traditional course of patterning the new flag from the French Tricolor and, instead, created a flag with five stripes to represent the five regions of the country. The white star represents hope; the red field, the blood that flowed in the struggle for independence; yellow, mining; and green, agriculture and hope. Another interpretation is that the yellow represents the peasants' faith in the importance of their chores; red, humanity, love, and loyalty; and white, purity.

| TOGO | |
|---|---|
| Official Name: | Republic of Togo |
| Capital: | Lomé |
| Languages: | French, indigenous |
| Religions: | Indigenous, Christian, Muslim |
| Exports: | Phosphates, cocoa, coffee, palm kernels |
| Imports: | Consumer goods, fuel, machinery, food |
| Highest Point: | 3,235 ft. (986 m) |
| Lowest Point: | Sea level |
| Area: | 21,925 sq. mi. (56,764 sq km) |

# BURKINA

Burkina Faso was, until a coup in 1983, called Upper Volta; it was under this former name that Burkina Faso hoisted its first flag in 1959. The country gained its independence from France the following year. This first flag had black, white, and red horizontal stripes, which represented the three branches of the Volta River, from which the country derived its name. After the Council for the National Revolution staged a coup in 1983, the country adopted a new name, a new flag bearing the pan-African colors, and a new revolutionary emblem. The pan-African colors are said to stand for the nation's solidarity with other former colonial states. The star represents the new guidelines set by the Council for the National Revolution.

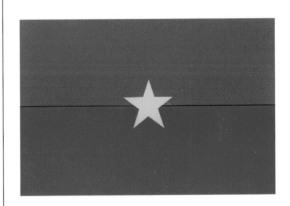

| BURKINA | |
|---|---|
| Official Name: | Burkina Faso |
| Capital: | Ouagadougou |
| Languages: | French, indigenous |
| Religions: | Animistic, Muslim, Christian |
| Exports: | Livestock, peanuts, shea nut products |
| Imports: | Food, fuels, transportation equipment, consumer goods |
| Highest Point: | 2,451 ft. (747 m) |
| Lowest Point: | 650 ft. (198 m) |
| Area: | 105,869 sq. mi. (274,094 sq km) |

# BENIN

In 1960, Dahomey received its independence from France. The flag the newly independent country hoisted included the pan-African colors, arranged with a green vertical stripe at the hoist and yellow-over-red horizontal stripes in the fly. The socialist revolution in 1975 altered the name of the country to Benin and a new flag—a red star in the upper hoist corner of a green field—was adopted. The end of the Marxist-Leninist regime in 1990 was symbolized by a reversion to the original national flag. The name of the country, however, remained the same.

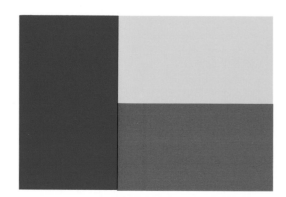

| **BENIN** | |
|---|---|
| Official Name: | People's Republic of Benin |
| Capital: | Porto-Novo |
| Languages: | French, Fon, Adja, indigenous |
| Religions: | Animistic, Christian, Muslim |
| Exports: | Palm products, cotton |
| Imports: | Clothing, consumer goods, construction materials |
| Highest Point: | 2,103 ft. (641 m) |
| Lowest Point: | Sea level |
| Area: | 43,484 sq. mi. (112,580 sq km) |

© Abbas/Leo de Wys, Inc.

# ZAIRE

Zaire, called Congo until 1971, had many flags before its current national flag. For many years after 1884, when Zaire was known as the Congo Free State, it flew a blue flag with a gold star, designed by British explorer Henry Stanley. In 1960, Belgian and Congolese leaders agreed upon independence for the country and Patrice Lumumba was appointed the first premier on June 21 of that year. At this time, six other stars were added in the hoist, but in 1963, the flag was altered; it retained the background but took on a red diagonal edged in yellow and a single yellow star in the canton. During the 1960s, the country was torn apart by several civil wars protesting outside influence, and each secessionist regime adopted its own flag. In 1971 the Mouvement Populaire de la Révolution (MPR) gained power; the country's name was changed to Zaire, and a new flag in the pan-African colors was adopted. This flag is basically the same as that of the MPR, except the arm and torch party emblem appears directly on the green field on the MPR flag. The lit torch symbolizes the struggle for freedom, while the green represents Zaire's hope for the future.

| **ZAIRE** | |
|---|---|
| Official Name: | Republic of Zaire |
| Capital: | Kinshasa |
| Languages: | French, Lingala, Swahili, Kikongo |
| Religions: | Roman Catholic, Protestant, Kimbanguist |
| Exports: | Copper, cobalt, diamonds, petroleum |
| Imports: | Petroleum products, food, machinery |
| Highest Point: | 16,763 ft. (5,109 m) |
| Lowest Point: | Sea level |
| Area: | 905,567 sq. mi. (2,344,512 sq km) |

CENTER: *A royal mask from Zaire. Traditional African societies have a rich heritage of artistic expression.*

# CONGO

A Marxist government ruled the Congo from 1969 until 1991. Its flag was red with a gold star, crossed hammer, and hoe with palm branches of green. The end of the people's republic regime saw the restoration of the original flag of the Congo, which had been adopted in 1959, when the nation gained its independence from France. The pan-African colors were arranged in diagonal stripes in order to distinguish them from similar colors used in horizontal or vertical combinations by other African nations. Those colors were originally used by the African Democratic Rally, which united the French territories in their struggle for self-government.

| CONGO | |
|---|---|
| Official Name: | Republic of the Congo |
| Capital: | Brazzaville |
| Languages: | French, indigenous |
| Religions: | Animistic, Christian, Muslim |
| Exports: | Petroleum, wood, coffee, cocoa |
| Imports: | Machinery, transportation equipment, consumer goods |
| Highest Point: | 2,963 ft. (903 m) |
| Lowest Point: | Sea level |
| Area: | 132,047 sq. mi. (341,870 sq km) |

# ZIMBABWE

Zimbabwe has had many flags in its history since the British, via Cecil Rhodes and the British South Africa Company, colonized this region in the 1890s. In 1923, Britain took control over the area, then called Southern Rhodesia, and the region flew British flags from 1924 until 1965, when Rhodesian prime minister Ian Smith announced his country's declaration of independence. This announcement was called the Unilateral Declaration of Independence (UDI), but the act was called illegal by the British, who demanded that Rhodesia broaden the voting rights to provide for the eventual rule by the majority Africans. At this time Rhodesia used a light blue flag with a Union Jack in the canton, which remained in use until 1968, when a flag of green-white-green with the arms of Rhodesia in the center replaced it. The green-and-white flag was replaced in 1979 by the flag of Zimbabwe-Rhodesia. On April 18, 1980, Zimbabwe became independent; its flag is based upon the colors of the leading political party, the Patriotic Front, and simultaneously reflects the colors of the pan-African movement. The bird of Zimbabwe, adopted from the arms, is a reminder of the ancient African city for which the nation is named.

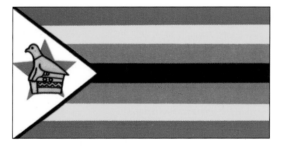

| ZIMBABWE | |
|---|---|
| Official Name: | Republic of Zimbabwe |
| Capital: | Harare |
| Languages: | English, Chishona, Ndebele |
| Religions: | Syncretic, Christian, indigenous |
| Exports: | Tobacco, asbestos, copper, tin, chrome |
| Imports: | Machinery, petroleum, transportation equipment |
| Highest Point: | 8,504 ft. (2,592 m) |
| Lowest Point: | 530 ft. (162 m) |
| Area: | 150,804 sq. mi. (390,432 sq km) |

*Victoria Falls, Zimbabwe, is one of the most impressive natural features on the African continent.*

# CHAD

Chad won its independence from France in 1960, but in fact has been an autonomous republic within the French Community since 1958. During this period of autonomy the flag of Chad was introduced: it is similar to the French Tricolor, except that yellow replaces white in the center band. This difference is the result of a conscious attempt to link the French colors with the pan-African ones. The blue represents the sky, hope, and life; the yellow, the sun shining over the nation; and the red, the spirit of the country.

| CHAD | |
|---|---|
| Official Name: | Republic of Chad |
| Capital: | N'Djamena |
| Languages: | French, Arabic, indigenous |
| Religions: | Muslim, indigenous, Christian |
| Exports: | Cotton, meat, fish |
| Imports: | Food, petroleum, machinery, motor vehicles |
| Highest Point: | 11,204 ft. (3,415 m) |
| Lowest Point: | 525 ft. (160 m) |
| Area: | 495,755 sq. mi. (1,283,510 sq km) |

# CENTRAL AFRICAN REPUBLIC

The Central African Republic won its independence from France in 1960, and its flag is a unique combination of the French Tricolor and the pan-African colors. This combination was adopted to symbolize the concept of a unified African nation joined with the French Community. While there is no official interpretation of the colors, possibly due to the constant power struggles in the country, the star symbolizes African freedom.

| CENTRAL AFRICAN REPUBLIC | |
|---|---|
| Official Name: | Central African Republic |
| Capital: | Bangui |
| Languages: | French, Sango |
| Religions: | Protestant, Roman Catholic, indigenous, Muslim |
| Exports: | Cotton, coffee, diamonds, wood |
| Imports: | Petroleum products, machinery |
| Highest Point: | 4,626 ft. (1,410 m) |
| Lowest Point: | 1,100 ft. (335 m) |
| Area: | 240,535 sq. mi. (622,745 sq km) |

*LEFT: Surprisingly, the black rhinoceros has never joined other wildlife as a common flag symbol.*

*TOP, RIGHT: A doorway in Tunisia. Moslem artists, forbidden to represent living beings, feature geometric patterns in their work.*

# TUNISIA

Tunisia sits at the site of ancient Carthage and was a former Barbary state (part of the Barbary Coast, a North African region dominated by pirates) under the control of Turkey (see **Turkey**). During the time of Turkish domination, many different flags, mostly red, green, and white, were used. After about 1800, a red flag with a crescent moon and a multipointed star served as the official flag. The present flag dates back to 1835, when the Bey Husein II, the ruler, introduced it to his troops. After a treaty signed in 1883, Tunisia became a French protectorate, and the Tunisian flag could be used only on land. In 1956, Tunisia became independent.

| TUNISIA | |
|---|---|
| Official Name: | Republic of Tunisia |
| Capital: | Tunis |
| Languages: | Arabic, French |
| Religions: | Muslim |
| Exports: | Petroleum, phosphates, olive oil |
| Imports: | Machinery, food |
| Highest Point: | 5,066 ft. (1,544 m) |
| Lowest Point: | -70 ft. (-21 m) |
| Area: | 63,170 sq. mi. (163,547 sq km) |

# ALGERIA

Algeria had many flags, most of which consisted of stripes of various colors, during the Barbary Coast pirate-raid days. The green and white colors of Algeria's current flag were associated with Abd-Al-Kadr, the Algerian national hero who fought French dominance during the 1840s. Abd-Al-Kadr's flags also included the Hand of Fatima, which still appears on the national emblem. According to legend, Massali Haj (the leader of the resistance movement against the French) designed the current flag in 1928. In 1954, a military campaign was launched by the Front de Libération Nationale, which used this flag during the struggle that eventually succeeded in winning Algeria's independence from France in 1962, at which point the flag became the country's official national flag.

The Algerian flag is unique, since its crescent is more closed than the crescents that appear on other Moslem countries' flags. Algerian belief says that the elongated horns of the crescent bring good fortune and happiness. The white of the flag is said to symbolize purity, while the green is said to be the favorite color of Muhammad.

| ALGERIA | |
| --- | --- |
| Official Name: | Democratic and Popular Republic of Algeria |
| Capital: | Algiers |
| Languages: | Arabic, Berber, French |
| Religions: | Sunni Muslim |
| Exports: | Petroleum, natural gas |
| Imports: | Equipment, semifinished goods, food |
| Highest Point: | 9,541 ft. (2,908 m) |
| Lowest Point: | -131 ft. (-40 m) |
| Area: | 919,595 sq. mi. (2,380,831 sq km) |

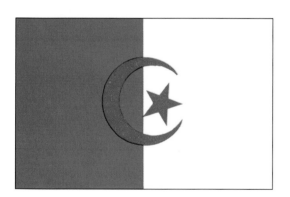

# MAURITANIA

Mauritania, while for many years claimed by Morocco, was a French West African province. The flag was introduced after the country became an autonomous republic within the French Community in 1958, and retained upon the country's independence in 1960. The flag's green color represents hope and prosperity. The crescent moon and star are Islamic symbols.

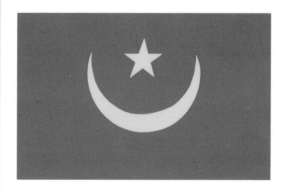

| MAURITANIA | |
| --- | --- |
| Official Name: | Islamic Republic of Mauritania |
| Capital: | Nouakchott |
| Languages: | Arabic, French |
| Religions: | Muslim |
| Exports: | Iron ore, processed fish |
| Imports: | Food, machinery, petroleum, consumer goods |
| Highest Point: | 3,002 ft. (915 m) |
| Lowest Point: | -10 ft. (-3 m) |
| Area: | 397,955 sq. mi. (1,030,305 sq km) |

# COMOROS

The Comoro Islands were controlled by Moslem sultans from 1843 to 1886, when they became a French colony. During Moslem occupation, the island flew various red flags; there was no single flag until 1963, when a flag of green with a crescent and four stars, each star representing one main island, was adopted. In 1974, a referendum favored independence, but Mayotte, the only Christian island, preferred to remain French. In 1975, upon independence, the crescent and stars were moved to the corner of the flag against a red background; there was a green stripe along the bottom edge of the flag. During this time, Mayotte decided to remain aligned with France, but its star was not struck from the flag. Following a pro-French military coup in 1978, the flag was altered to the present design.

| COMOROS | |
| --- | --- |
| Official Name: | Federal Islamic Republic of the Comoros |
| Capital: | Moroni |
| Languages: | Arabic, French, Swahili |
| Religions: | Shirazi Muslim, Roman Catholic |
| Exports: | Perfume oils, vanilla, copra, cloves |
| Imports: | Rice, fuels, textiles, machinery |
| Highest Point: | 7,746 ft. (2,361 m) |
| Lowest Point: | Sea level |
| Area: | 838 sq. mi. (2,170 sq km) |

# MOROCCO

Morocco has been ruled by the Hassani dynasty since 1649. Morocco was divided into French and Spanish protectorates from 1912 to 1956, with Tangier serving as the international city as of 1923. When the French modernized their section's army in 1915, they added a green Seal of Solomon, also an ancient magical device, to the country's plain red flag. During this forty-four-year period, each protectorate had its own flag for internal and external use. French Morocco could use the red flag with the green pentagram only on land, but when Morocco became an independent and reunified nation in 1956, this became the national flag.

| MOROCCO | |
|---|---|
| Official Name: | Kingdom of Morocco |
| Capital: | Rabat |
| Languages: | Arabic, Berber dialects, French |
| Religions: | Muslim |
| Exports: | Phosphates, food, consumer goods |
| Imports: | Petroleum, food, machinery |
| Highest Point: | 13,665 ft. (4,165 m) |
| Lowest Point: | -180 ft. (-55 m) |
| Area: | 172,414 sq. mi. (446,380 sq km) |

*The Royal Palais Ambass in Rabat, Morocco, is one of Africa's last royal residences.*

# LIBYA

Libya's flag has changed many times since the country attained independence from Allied occupation (it was formerly ruled by Italy) in 1951. Initially, Libya's flag, based on the black flag of Idris Es-senussi, was bordered by red and green, and had a star and crescent at its center. After Colonel Mu'ammar-Muhammad al-Qaddafi took power in 1969, the flag changed to the red, white, and black colors of the Arab liberation movement, only to change again in 1972 to the flag of the Federation of Arab Republics, which was similar to Egypt's current flag. However, in 1977, after Egypt and Israel attempted peace, Libya left the Federation and changed its flag to the present plain green flag, which, today, is the world's only flag of a solid color. The green symbolizes the concept of *Jamahiriya,* or mass participation, and Colonel Qaddafi's "Green Revolution."

| LIBYA | |
|---|---|
| Official Name: | Socialist People's Libyan Arab Jamahiriya |
| Capital: | Tripoli |
| Languages: | Arabic |
| Religions: | Sunni Muslim |
| Exports: | Petroleum |
| Imports: | Machinery, transportation equipment, manufactured goods |
| Highest Point: | 7,434 ft. (2,266 m) |
| Lowest Point: | -138 ft. (-42 m) |
| Area: | 679,362 sq. mi. (1,758,868 sq km) |

© Steve Vidler/Leo de Wys, Inc.

# DJIBOUTI

Djibouti, dominated by the French since 1862, was formerly known as the Territory of the Afars (ethnically related to Ethiopians) and the Issas (related to the Somalis). Before that, the country was known as French Somaliland. The blue color of its flag was that of the Somali-led nationalist groups, while the green and white were those of rival Afar groups. In 1972, the two groups united in the People's African Independence League; the League combined the two groups' colors into one flag, which was hoisted upon independence in 1977. Today, the colors have the following official explanation: blue represents the sea; green, the earth; white, peace; and red, unity.

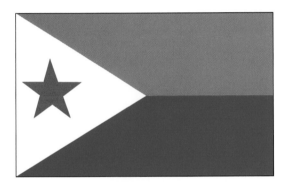

| DJIBOUTI | |
|---|---|
| Official Name: | Republic of Djibouti |
| Capital: | Djibouti |
| Languages: | French, Somali, Afar, Arabic |
| Religions: | Muslim, Christian |
| Exports: | Hides and skins, coffee |
| Imports: | Machinery, food, transportation equipment, textiles |
| Highest Point: | 6,768 ft. (2,063 m) |
| Lowest Point: | -509 ft. (-155 m) |
| Area: | 8,880 sq. mi. (2,990 sq km) |

*TOP, CENTER: The cheetah serves as part of the coat of arms of Somalia.*

# SOMALIA

Somalia, formerly Italian Somaliland, adopted its flag while the country was a United Nations trusteeship territory. Accordingly, Somalia adapted the blue field of the United Nations flag and placed a white star in the center. The star symbolizes unity and the five points represent the five regions in which its natives, the Somalis, reside: the former Italian and British Somalilands, which comprise the present republic; Ethiopia; French Somaliland (now Djibouti); and northern Kenya. When the region became independent in 1960, the Italian and British Somalilands were united into what is now known as Somalia.

| SOMALIA | |
|---|---|
| Official Name: | Somali Democratic Republic |
| Capital: | Mogadishu |
| Languages: | Somali, Arabic, English, Italian |
| Religions: | Sunni Muslim |
| Exports: | Livestock, bananas, hides and skins |
| Imports: | Food, petroleum products, transportation equipment |
| Highest Point: | 7,897 ft. (2,407 m) |
| Lowest Point: | Sea level |
| Area: | 246,200 sq. mi. (637,412 sq km) |

# ANGOLA

Angola is one of several African countries whose flag was adapted from the flag of a dominant political party during liberation. In the case of Angola, this party was the Movimento Popular de Libertaçao de Angola (often referred to as the Popular Movement), a Soviet-backed group who rallied around a red-over-black flag with a large yellow star in its center. Red and black are linked with the flags used by the July 26 Movement in Cuba and the Sandinistas in Nicaragua, and are meant to express the idea of "Liberty or Death," an extremely popular liberation sentiment also echoed in early flags of the United States. In 1975, Angola won independence from the Portuguese.

The current official interpretation of the colors is as follows: red symbolizes the blood spilled in the struggle for freedom; black, the African continent; and the yellow star stands for the country's vast natural resources. The symbols of the cogwheel and the machete respectively represent industry and agriculture.

| ANGOLA | |
|---|---|
| Official Name: | People's Republic of Angola |
| Capital: | Luanda |
| Languages: | Portuguese, indigenous |
| Religions: | Animistic, Roman Catholic, Protestant |
| Exports: | Petroleum, coffee, diamonds |
| Imports: | Capital equipment, wine, iron, steel |
| Highest Point: | 8,596 ft. (2,620 m) |
| Lowest Point: | Sea level |
| Area: | 481,353 sq. mi. (1,246,227 sq km) |

## MOZAMBIQUE

Mozambique gained independence from Portuguese domination in 1975, led by the Frente de Libertaçao de Moçambique (FRELIMO). Prior to independence, FRELIMO's flag resembled the current national flag, minus the emblems in the red triangle. Upon independence, a new flag was introduced that used the same party colors but laid them out differently—the stripes were in the form of sunbeams commencing in the upper hoist, on top of which was a simplified form of the national arms. In 1983, FRELIMO adopted a new flag, and FRELIMO's original party flag was adopted as the new national flag. The hoe and Kalashnikov rifle serve as emblems of agricultural defense, and the star symbolizes socialism.

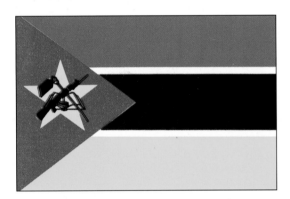

| MOZAMBIQUE | |
|---|---|
| Official Name: | Republic of Mozambique |
| Capital: | Maputo |
| Languages: | Portuguese, indigenous |
| Religions: | Indigenous, Christian, Muslim |
| Exports: | Cashews, shrimp, sugar, tea, cotton |
| Imports: | Machinery, petroleum, motor vehicles |
| Highest Point: | 7,992 ft. (2,436 m) |
| Lowest Point: | Sea level |
| Area: | 302,329 sq. mi. (782,730 sq km) |

## TANZANIA

Tanzania's national flag is a combination of two different political parties' flags. The green and black were the colors of the Tanganyika African National Union (TANU), which led Tanzania, then called Tanganyika, from United Nations protectorate status under Britain to independence in 1961. In January 1964, after centuries of Arab dominance, the Afro-Shirazi party took over the island of Zanzibar (Zanzibar is often referred to as the island of cloves because the chief product is cloves and clove oil, and lies twenty-three miles [37 m] off the coast of Tanzania) and overthrew the sultan. The Afro-Shirazi party's flag consisted of horizontal stripes—blue, black, and green—with a yellow hoe in the center. Several months later, in June, after Zanzibar linked with Tanganyika, the blue from its flag was added to the green, black, and yellow of Tanganyika's flag. The colors were arranged diagonally to signify that they were of equal importance.

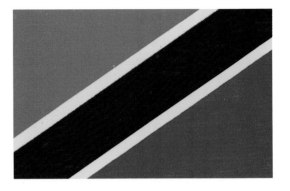

| TANZANIA | |
|---|---|
| Official Name: | United Republic of Tanzania |
| Capital: | Dar es Salaam |
| Languages: | Swahili, English, indigenous |
| Religions: | Christian, Muslim, indigenous |
| Exports: | Coffee, cotton, sisal, cashews, diamonds |
| Imports: | Manufactured goods, machinery, transportation equipment, petroleum |
| Highest Point: | 19,340 ft. (5,895 m) |
| Lowest Point: | Sea level |
| Area: | 364,900 sq. mi. (944,726 sq km) |

*The Ngorongoro Crater is one of Tanzania's greatest landmarks.*

*TANGANYIKA TERRITORY; STATE ENSIGN 1919–1961*

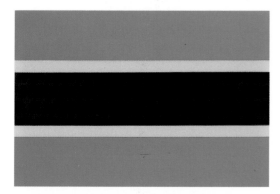

*REPUBLIC OF TANGANYIKA; NATIONAL FLAG 1961–1964*

*SULTANATE OF ZANZIBAR; NATIONAL FLAG 1963–1964*

*ABOVE: The lion is the most popular of all heraldic beasts.*

*BELOW: Few birds have the grace and beauty of the flamingo.*

# UGANDA

Uganda was granted independence from Britain in 1962, and its national symbols have remained the same since that time—despite a rather violent history. The proposed flag was in the colors of the rival Democratic party at the time of independence, but was quickly changed before the official day. This design is still used today. The crested crane, which appears in the white center circle, was the former colonial badge.

Before independence, Uganda was divided into several African kingdoms (which were finally suppressed in 1966). Each of these kingdoms had its own flag; these flags often bore the traditional symbol of the monarch, the drum.

| UGANDA | |
|---|---|
| Official Name: | Republic of Uganda |
| Capital: | Kampala |
| Languages: | English, Swahili, Luganda, indigenous |
| Religions: | Roman Catholic, Protestant, Muslim, indigenous |
| Exports: | Coffee, cotton, tea |
| Imports: | Petroleum products, machinery, textiles |
| Highest Point: | 16,763 ft. (5,109 m) |
| Lowest Point: | 2,000 ft. (610 m) |
| Area: | 91,134 sq. mi. (235,946 sq km) |

# *SEYCHELLES*

The Seychelles were ruled by Britain as a part of Mauritius from 1814 until 1903, when these islands became a separate colony. Due to pressure from the United Nations, the Seychelles won their independence in 1976 and adopted a flag in the colors of the former Democratic party, blue and white, combined with the colors of the Seychelles People's United party (SPUP, currently the People's Progressive Front), which were red and white. This flag was in the shape of a white saltire dividing equal triangles of blue and red. In 1977, there was a socialist coup; SPUP seized power and outlawed all political parties except itself. SPUP hoisted a new flag based completely on its party flag, which is identical to the present national flag, but has a yellow rising sun.

| SEYCHELLES | |
| --- | --- |
| Official Name: | Republic of Seychelles |
| Capital: | Victoria |
| Languages: | English, French |
| Religions: | Roman Catholic |
| Exports: | Copra, cinnamon, vanilla, fish |
| Imports: | Food, manufactured goods, machinery, petroleum |
| Highest Point: | 2,970 ft. (905 m) |
| Lowest Point: | Sea level |
| Area: | 171 sq. mi. (443 sq km) |

# *BURUNDI*

Burundi, one of the poorest and most densely populated countries in Africa, has seen, in its various flag emblems, changes that reflect the nation's political climate. The flag was first designed in 1962, when Burundi, liberated from Belgium, became an independent kingdom. At that time, the flag featured the drum *Karyenda*, the traditional symbol of the monarchy. In front of *Karyenda* appeared a sorghum plant, the country's principal food. In 1966, the crown prince overthrew the Mwami (king), and captured the royal drum. The prince was then himself deposed by the prime minister, who declared the monarchy dead, and *Karyenda* was then removed from the flag. In 1967, the present design was adopted; its three center stars signify the words of the national motto: Unity, Work, Progress. The dark red symbolizes the victims of the freedom struggle; green, progress and hope; and white, peace.

| BURUNDI | |
| --- | --- |
| Official Name: | Republic of Burundi |
| Capital: | Usumbura |
| Languages: | Kirundi, French |
| Religions: | Roman Catholic, Protestant, indigenous, Muslim |
| Exports: | Coffee, tea, cotton |
| Imports: | Textiles, food, transportation equipment |
| Highest Point: | 9,055 ft. (2,760 m) |
| Lowest Point: | 2,534 ft. (772 m) |
| Area: | 10,747 sq. mi. (27,824 sq km) |

# *ZAMBIA*

Zambia was called Northern Rhodesia until independence in 1964. At that time, the United National Independence party (UNIP) took power and adopted a flag that uses its colors. UNIP remained in power until 1991, but has changed the design of its flag by removing the soaring eagle and replacing it with a hoe in the center with the word *unity*. The national flag, however, has remained the same. The unusual orange-colored stripe represents the country's chief mineral, copper (see **Cyprus**). The soaring eagle, which represents freedom, is a carryover from the years when Zambia was controlled by its white minority. At that time, the eagle appeared on the nation's arms.

| ZAMBIA | |
| --- | --- |
| Official Name: | Republic of Zambia |
| Capital: | Lusaka |
| Languages: | English, indigenous |
| Religions: | Christian, Muslim, Hindu, indigenous |
| Exports: | Copper, cobalt, zinc, lead, tobacco |
| Imports: | Machinery, transportation equipment, manufactured goods |
| Highest Point: | 7,100 ft. (2,164 m) |
| Lowest Point: | 1,081 ft. (329 m) |
| Area: | 290,586 sq. mi. (752,327 sq km) |

# LESOTHO

Lesotho, once called Basutoland, gained its independence from Britain in 1966. Lesotho's original flag, adopted at this time, was in the blue, white, red, and green colors of the dominant political party, the Lesotho National party (LNP). After a 1986 coup, the LNP lost control of the government and the flag was altered to make it more politically neutral in appearance. The diagonal stripes are meant to signify the national motto: Peace (white), Rain (blue), Plenty (green). The stylized brown silhouette of a shield, spear, and knobkerrie (a stick used as a club by tribesmen) symbolize the people's willingness to defend the nation.

| LESOTHO | |
|---|---|
| Official Name: | Kingdom of Lesotho |
| Capital: | Maseru |
| Languages: | English, Sesotho, Zulu, Xhosa |
| Religions: | Christian, indigenous |
| Exports: | Wool, mohair, food |
| Imports: | Food, construction material, clothing |
| Highest Point: | 11,424 ft. (3,482 m) |
| Lowest Point: | Sea level |
| Area: | 11,720 sq. mi. (30,343 sq km) |

# BOTSWANA

Botswana was called Bechuanaland until its independence from Britain in 1966. Its flag is meant to symbolize both the country's dependence on *Pula* (life-giving rain) and the coexistence of black and white Africans. Perhaps because both countries rely heavily on raising livestock, Botswana shares with Lesotho (see **Lesotho**) the symbolism of blue for *Pula*.

| BOTSWANA | |
|---|---|
| Official Name: | Republic of Botswana |
| Capital: | Gaborone |
| Languages: | English, Setswana |
| Religions: | Indigenous, Christian |
| Exports: | Diamonds, cattle, animal products |
| Imports: | Food, machinery, motor vehicles, petroleum |
| Highest Point: | 4,886 ft. (1,489 m) |
| Lowest Point: | 1,684 ft. (513 m) |
| Area: | 231,805 sq. mi. (600,143 sq km) |

*Botswana has attempted to preserve the giraffe and other animals facing extinction.*

© Tim Gibson/Envision

# THE GAMBIA

The Gambia was, in 1588, Britain's first African possession. In 1965, The Gambia gained independence and adopted its flag, designed by the English College of Arms. The flag is purely neutral; it has no political allegiance or roots. A Gambian, a Mr. L. Thomasi, thought of the idea for the flag and interpreted its colors as follows: red represents the shining sun; blue, the River Gambia, for which the country is named; green, agriculture; and white, peace and purity. Surrounded on three sides by Senegal, The Gambia, one of Africa's few functioning democracies, formed a confederation with its neighbor from 1982 to 1989, but neither country's national symbols was altered.

| THE GAMBIA | |
|---|---|
| Official Name: | Republic of The Gambia |
| Capital: | Banjul |
| Languages: | English, indigenous |
| Religions: | Muslim, Christian |
| Exports: | Peanuts and peanut products, fish |
| Imports: | Manufactured goods, machinery, food |
| Highest Point: | 150 ft. (46 m) |
| Lowest Point: | Sea level |
| Area: | 4,361 sq. mi. (11,291 sq km) |

# SWAZILAND

Swaziland, one of Africa's last ruling dynasties, uses a flag that is similar to that of The Gambia, even though it was not designed by the English College of Arms. The flag originally was the flag of the Emasotsha Regiment of the Swazi Pioneer Corps. The shield displays the pattern of the regiment, a tassel of *ligwalagwala* (lourie) and *lisaka-buli* (widowbird) feathers. The shield sits in front of two spears and a staff that carries feather tassels *(tinjobo)*. Swaziland won its independence from Britain in 1968.

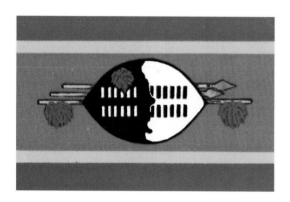

| SWAZILAND | |
|---|---|
| Official Name: | Kingdom of Swaziland |
| Capital: | Mbabane |
| Languages: | English, Swazi |
| Religions: | Christian, indigenous |
| Exports: | Sugar, asbestos, wood products, fruits |
| Imports: | Motor vehicles, petroleum products, machinery |
| Highest Point: | 6,109 ft. (1,862 m) |
| Lowest Point: | 70 ft. (21 m) |
| Area: | 6,704 sq. mi. (17,357 sq km) |

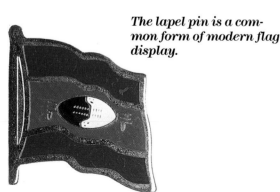

*The lapel pin is a common form of modern flag display.*

# MADAGASCAR

Madagascar, settled two thousand years ago by Malayan-Indonesian people, was ruled by the Imérina monarchy until 1896, when its queen was deposed and it became French-occupied. During rule under the monarchy, the nation used flags of red and white. In fact, the national flag, created in 1958, two years before independence, seems to have been inspired by the flag of Queen Ranavalona, which was white with a red square panel and the crowned initials 'RM.' The nationalist movement of 1947 also used red and white on its flag. In addition, the national flag of Madagascar also has a green panel to represent the nation's minority coastal people.

| MADAGASCAR | |
|---|---|
| Official Name: | Democratic Republic of Madagascar |
| Capital: | Antananarivo |
| Languages: | Malagasy, French |
| Religions: | Indigenous, Christian, Muslim |
| Exports: | Coffee, vanilla, sugar, cloves |
| Imports: | Consumer goods, food, machinery, petroleum |
| Highest Point: | 9,436 ft. (2,876 m) |
| Lowest Point: | Sea level |
| Area: | 226,658 sq. mi. (586,818 sq km) |

*Hundreds of lemur species live on the island of Madagascar.*

# CÔTE D'IVOIRE

Côte d'Ivoire's name (formerly the Ivory Coast) is derived from the ivory trade that used to thrive within its boundaries. Although it became independent from France in 1960, Côte d'Ivoire adopted a flag modeled after the French Tricolor and was opposed to integrating with other African nations that did not have a link with France. In fact, in 1986, it was officially decreed that its French name was the only official name. The orange of the flag represents the savannah of the country's northern region, while the green represents its southern coastal region.

**CÔTE D'IVOIRE**

| | |
|---|---|
| Official Name: | Republic of Côte d'Ivoire |
| Capital: | Yamoussoukro |
| Languages: | French, indigenous |
| Religions: | Indigenous, Muslim, Christian |
| Exports: | Cocoa, coffee, wood |
| Imports: | Machinery, petroleum, motor vehicles |
| Highest Point: | 5,748 ft. (1,752 m) |
| Lowest Point: | Sea level |
| Area: | 123,847 sq. mi. (320,640 sq km) |

*A Bakora mask from Côte d'Ivoire.*

# NIGER

Niger and Côte d'Ivoire share a similar history. Both countries became independent from France in August 1960 and adopted their flags at the same time. Both countries were determined to continue their links with France. The colors of Niger's flag are officially explained the same way as Côte d'Ivoire's: the orange represents its savannah, and the green represents the fertile southern region of the nation. However, in Niger's flag, the white stripe represents purity, and the orange disk stands for the sun.

**NIGER**

| | |
|---|---|
| Official Name: | Republic of Niger |
| Capital: | Niamey |
| Languages: | French, Hausa, indigenous |
| Religions: | Muslim, indigenous, Christian |
| Exports: | Uranium, livestock, vegetables |
| Imports: | Petroleum, machinery, motor vehicles |
| Highest Point: | 6,634 ft. (2,022 m) |
| Lowest Point: | 200 ft. (61 m) |
| Area: | 489,191 sq. mi. (1,266,515 sq km) |

# GABON

Gabon, one of Africa's most prosperous countries, sought and won in August 1960, much like Côte d'Ivoire and Niger, independence from France, without any local affiliations. Consequently, Gabon avoided using the pan-African colors. The country's original flag was selected in 1959; its center yellow stripe was one-half its current width, and there was a French Tricolor in the canton. Upon independence, the present flag was adopted.

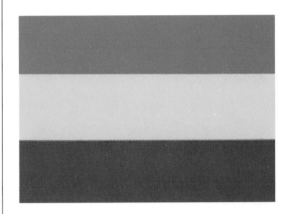

**GABON**

| | |
|---|---|
| Official Name: | Gabonese Republic |
| Capital: | Libreville |
| Languages: | French, indigenous |
| Religions: | Christian, Muslim, animistic |
| Exports: | Petroleum, wood and wood products, minerals |
| Imports: | Machinery, electrical equipment, transportation equipment |
| Highest Point: | 3,346 ft. (1,020 m) |
| Lowest Point: | Sea level |
| Area: | 103,347 sq. mi. (267,565 sq km) |

## EQUATORIAL GUINEA

Equatorial Guinea, a tract of land on the African continent and five islands off the coast of Cameroon, became independent from Spain in 1968 and adopted its flag the same day. The blue triangle symbolizes the sea; the green stripe, the nation's natural resources; the white stripe, peace; and the red stripe, the fight for independence. In the center of the flag are the nation's arms, which show a god-tree, adopted from the arms of Bata, a chief port. The stars symbolize the mainland and the five islands (Bioko, Annobón, Corisco, Elobey Grande, and Elobey Chico). The country's motto, *Unidad, Paz, Justicia* (Unity, Peace, Justice) appears in the scroll at the bottom of the arms.

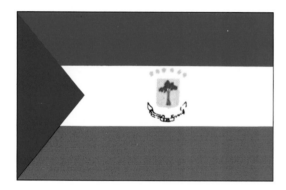

| EQUATORIAL GUINEA | |
|---|---|
| Official Name: | Republic of Equatorial Guinea |
| Capital: | Malabo |
| Languages: | Spanish, English, indigenous |
| Religions: | Roman Catholic, Protestant, animistic |
| Exports: | Cocoa, wood, coffee |
| Imports: | Food, petroleum, machinery, textiles |
| Highest Point: | 9,868 ft. (3,008 m) |
| Lowest Point: | Sea level |
| Area: | 10,831 sq. mi. (28,041 sq km) |

## SIERRA LEONE

Sierra Leone's capital city, Freetown, was founded in 1787 by the British government as a haven for freed African slaves. In 1951, the country's constitution was ratified, and in 1961, when independence was achieved, the country's arms, designed by the English College of Arms, were adopted. The national flag was designed afterward; it is a simple tricolor utilizing the main colors of the arms. The flag's colors are interpreted as follows: blue represents the sea; white, peace and justice; and green, agricultural economy.

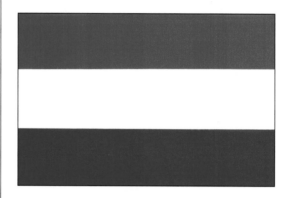

| SIERRA LEONE | |
|---|---|
| Official Name: | Republic of Sierra Leone |
| Capital: | Freetown |
| Languages: | English, Krio, indigenous |
| Religions: | Indigenous, Muslim, Christian |
| Exports: | Diamonds, palm kernels, coffee, cocoa |
| Imports: | Machinery, food, petroleum, transportation equipment |
| Highest Point: | 6,381 ft. (1,945 m) |
| Lowest Point: | Sea level |
| Area: | 27,925 sq. mi. (72,298 sq km) |

## NIGERIA

Nigeria won its independence from Britain in 1960. Its national flag was the result of a competition. The original design, submitted by Taiwo Akinkunmi, a student, had a red sun in the white stripe, but the symbol was omitted by the judges. The green of the flag symbolizes the land; the white represents peace and unity.

In 1967, the eastern region of Nigeria seceded and became the Republic of Biafra. Biafra has its own flag, a horizontal tricolor of red, black, and green (pan-African design) with a rising sun in the middle.

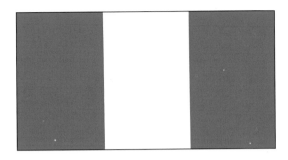

*Moslem warriors from northern Nigeria deck their horses in elaborate trappings.*

| NIGERIA | |
|---|---|
| Official Name: | Federal Republic of Nigeria |
| Capital: | Abuja |
| Languages: | English, Hausa, Yoruba, Ibo |
| Religions: | Muslim, Christian, indigenous |
| Exports: | Petroleum, cocoa, palm products |
| Imports: | Machinery |
| Highest Point: | 6,700 ft. (2,042 m) |
| Lowest Point: | Sea level |
| Area: | 356,669 sq. mi. (923,416 sq km) |

# LIBERIA

Liberia (the "Land of the Free") was set up as a settlement in 1821 by the American Colonization Society as a safe refuge for freed slaves. In 1827, Liberia adopted its first flag, which resembled the Stars and Stripes of the United States, except that it had a white cross instead of stars. In 1847, Liberia became an independent nation and adopted the present version of its flag. The eleven stripes symbolize the eleven signatures that appear on the Liberian Declaration of Independence. The blue field at the canton represents the continent of Africa. The star symbolizes the fact that, at the time of independence, Liberia was the only African-controlled republic on the African continent.

| LIBERIA | |
|---|---|
| Official Name: | Republic of Liberia |
| Capital: | Monrovia |
| Languages: | English, indigenous |
| Religions: | Indigenous, Muslim, Christian |
| Exports: | Iron ore, natural rubber, diamonds, wood |
| Imports: | Machinery, petroleum, transportation equipment, food |
| Highest Point: | 4,528 ft. (1,380 m) |
| Lowest Point: | Sea level |
| Area: | 43,000 sq. mi. (111,327 sq km) |

# SOUTH AFRICA

South Africa, the last African nation to be ruled by a white minority, was colonized by the Dutch in the early 1600s. After years of fighting with the British, the Boers ceded all other territories and, in 1910, formed the Union of South Africa—but the new country did not adopt a national flag until 1928 due to Anglo-Dutch conflicts. In an attempt at reconciliation, the British Union Flag, the flag of the Transvaal, and the flag of the Orange Free State were placed on the white stripe of the original Dutch tricolor. South Africa's flag is similar in design to the ancient *Prinsenvlag* used by William of Orange and the sixteenth-century Dutch freedom fighters. Until 1957, the British Union Flag was hoisted jointly with this flag.

It is widely believed that in the near future South Africa will change its government. This major shift, from white-minority government to African rule, will undoubtedly cause a change in the nation's flag. Should this occur, it is possible that the flag of the African National Congress, the leading African political party, may become a model for the new flag.

| SOUTH AFRICA | |
|---|---|
| Official Name: | Republic of South Africa |
| Capital: | Pretoria and Cape Town |
| Languages: | Afrikaans, English, indigenous |
| Religions: | Christian |
| Exports: | Gold, wool, diamonds |
| Imports: | Motor vehicles, machinery, metals |
| Highest Point: | 11,306 ft. (3,446 m) |
| Lowest Point: | Sea level |
| Area: | 433,680 sq. mi. (1,122,798 sq km) |

*RIGHT: The Cape of Good Hope is Africa's southernmost point.*

*BELOW: Cape Town shares with Pretoria joint status as capital of South Africa.*

*NATIONAL FLAG; 1927–TODAY*

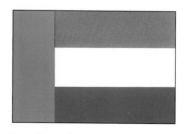

*ORANGE FREE STATE; NATIONAL FLAG 1856–1902*

*SOUTH AFRICAN REPUBLIC; NATIONAL FLAG 1858–1874, 1875–1877, 1880–1902*

*UNION OF SOUTH AFRICA; NATIONAL FLAG 1910–1928*

# NAMIBIA

Namibia, formerly South West Africa, was discovered by the Portuguese explorer Diaz in the late seventeenth century. In 1884 the country became a German colony and remained so until 1915 when it was taken by South Africa; in 1920 it became a South African mandate under the Treaty of Versailles. In 1974, under a United Nations Security Council resolution, South Africa was required to transfer power to the Namibians. Against the wishes of the United Nations, South Africa endorsed an all-white government in 1977. But in June of that year, at the urging of the United States, Great Britain, France, West Germany, and Canada, that government was dismantled and negotiations with the South-West African People's Organization (SWAPO) began. After years of rioting and confrontations, Namibia won the right to hold democratic elections in November 1989. SWAPO won the majority and in February 1990, SWAPO leader Sam Nujoma was elected president.

The Namibian flag is patterned slightly after the SWAPO flag, but reflects the independent stance of Africa's newest nation.

| | NAMIBIA |
|---|---|
| Official Name: | Republic of Namibia |
| Capital: | Windhoek |
| Languages: | English, Afrikaans, Oshivambo, at least twelve tribal languages |
| Religions: | Vary from tribe to tribe |
| Exports: | Mining, agriculture, fishing |
| Imports: | Foodstuffs, clothing, machinery, transportation equipment |
| Highest Point: | 8,442 ft. (2,573 m) |
| Lowest Point: | Sea level |
| Area: | 317,817 sq. mi. (823,146 sq km) |

*BELOW: This mural was painted by the people of Namibia. It appears at the Namibia Craft Center in Windhoek.*

© Jason Lauré

© Jason Lauré

*RIGHT: The modern city of Windhoek is the capital of Namibia.*

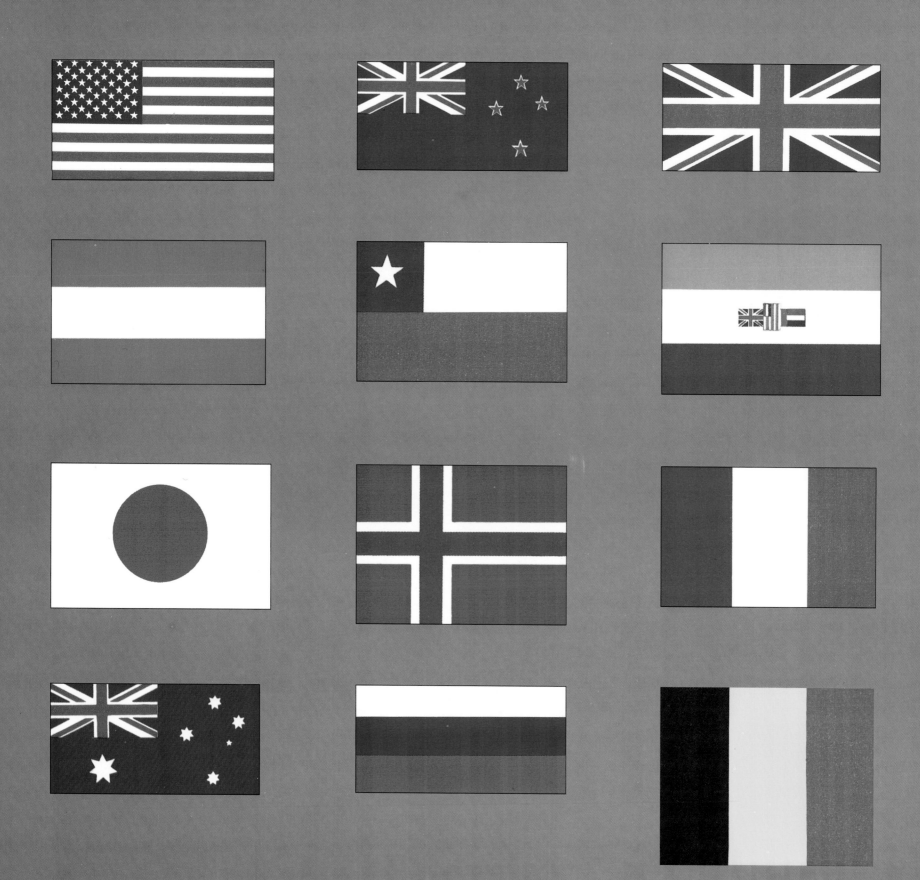

# CHAPTER TWO

# *Antarctica*

Antarctica is the continent surrounding the South Pole. The continent is comprised of frozen tundra, has no indigenous people, and was first explored in 1773–1775, when Captain James Cook of Britain reached 71°10′ South. Many landmarks and seas bear the names of the early explorers, such as Charles Wilkes of the United States, who followed the continent's coast for fifteen hundred miles (2,400 km) in 1840. Several explorers from countries as diverse as Norway, France, and the Soviet Union also have contributed to the exploration of this frozen continent.

From 1955 to 1957, the United States Navy, led by Admiral Richard Byrd, conducted Operation Deep Freeze, which supported the United States' scientific efforts for the International Geophysical Year of 1957. The operation, actually commanded by Rear Admiral George Dufek, established five coastal stations fronting the Indian, Pacific, and Atlantic oceans. Three interior stations were also created, and more than one million square miles (2,600,000 sq km) were explored in Wilkes Land (named for the aforementioned explorer). During the International Geophysical Year of 1957 and into 1958, scientists from twelve countries (Argentina, Australia, Belgium, Chile, France, Japan, New Zealand, Norway, South Africa, the Soviet Union, the United

Kingdom, and the United States) conducted important programs of Antarctic research. A network of some sixty stations on the continent and sub-Antarctic islands gathered information on a variety of topics: oceanography, glaciology, meteorology, seismology, geomagnetism, the ionosphere, cosmic rays, aurora, and airglow.

Because of this international effort, the twelve nations involved in the project signed in 1959 a thirty-year treaty that suspended any territorial claims and reserved the continent for research. Because there are no territorial claims on this continent, there are no flags for the region. Each of these twelve countries uses its own flag when exploring the area.

In 1962, the British Antarctic Territory was created from the southernmost British dependencies in the Falkland Islands. This territory is made up of the South Shetland Islands, the South Orkney Islands, and Graham Land. British Natural Environment Research vessels, to signal their intent, fly a specific flag when surveying the region. This flag is a blue ensign with a white shield. The upper section of the shield is crossed with blue waves. Over them is a gold torch, superimposed upon a red triangle. This shield displays the intentions of the British Antarctic Territory. The blue wavy lines symbolize the ice field and the sea. The torch symbolizes knowledge.

Until the distant future, when and if there are, at least, semipermanent colonies in the area, there is no need to fly anything other than national colors in this remote and desolate region.

*ABOVE: Antarctica is home to the emperor penguin, shown here.*

*RIGHT: Flags have been carried in human adventures throughout history.*

*ABOVE: In 1860 an Anglo-American expedition visited Antarctic waters.*

*BELOW: Some icebergs are larger than some small countries.*

**AUSTRALIA**

**BELGIUM**

**FRANCE**

**NEW ZEALAND**

**SOUTH AFRICA**

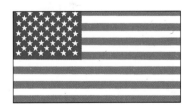

**UNITED STATES OF AMERICA**

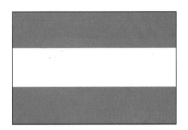

**ARGENTINA**

**CHILE**

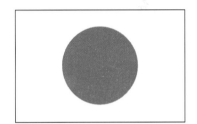

**JAPAN**

**NORWAY**

**RUSSIA**

**UNITED KINGDOM**

*Scientific expeditions can learn much from the unspoiled Antarctic environment.*

*LEFT: One artist's interpretation of the Antarctic continent as discovered by Commodore Wilkes.*

*BOTTOM, LEFT: Icebergs form from chunks of ice cap that have broken off from glaciers and ice shells.*

*BELOW: The penguin is featured in the coat of arms of Argentine Antarctica.*

# CHAPTER THREE

# *Asia*

The continent of Asia has been called the land of enchantment, which is no small wonder, for this continent is extremely diverse. Asia is home to Arab nations as well as to the island country of Japan; and its boundaries include countries as different as Israel and Nepal. Additionally, the history of many of the countries on the Asian continent spans centuries. Likewise, many of Asia's national flags have histories that date back to the earliest of times as well as utilize symbols that are as varied as the people they represent.

In Chinese thought, for example, the world is divided into five realms: the Center (symbolized by the color yellow), the North (black), the South (red), the West (white), and the East (blue). For the Chinese, the dragon emblem also symbolizes the East. Such symbology is echoed in many flags, including those of China, Nepal, and South Korea. The symbols of the crescent and star of Islam are seen on the flags of many nations where Islam is practiced. Japan, a nation closed to the world for centuries, did without a national flag until it began to open its doors to the West in 1853, with the visit of United States Commodore Matthew Perry. This visit led to the revival of one of the country's oldest symbols, the sun disk. Also, there is the flag of Nepal, which, in its shape, differs from any other flag in use in the world today.

Asia is, indeed, a land of enchantment and wonder.

# TURKEY

Turkey has been an independent country since 1296, but did not become a republic until 1923. Today, most of Turkey is situated in Asia, but its former capital city, Byzantium, is in Europe. Legend has it that an attempt by Philip of Macedon to destroy the walls of Byzantium was discovered and thwarted because of the moonlight. Consequently, the moon became the city's emblem and has remained so even as Byzantium evolved into Constantinople and then, eventually, into Istanbul. It is also said that many centuries after the thwarted attack on the city, the Turkish sultan Osman had a vision in which he saw the crescent moon. Certainly, these two stories may be true or false; nevertheless, the national flag of Turkey displays the crescent moon and star that have represented the religion of Islam since at least the fifteenth century. Also, the color red has been associated with the Osmanli Turks since before their conquest of the Byzantine Empire and their consequent responsibility for the Caliphate, the spiritual leadership of Islam. The red fez is also a symbol of this leadership.

The flag of Turkey has been a model for many Moslem countries from southeast Asia to western Africa. In Moslem countries, using the crescent and star of Islam is believed to bring good fortune.

| TURKEY | |
|---|---|
| Official Name: | Republic of Turkey |
| Capital: | Ankara |
| Languages: | Turkish, Kurdish |
| Religions: | Muslim |
| Exports: | Cotton, tobacco, fruits, nuts, food |
| Imports: | Petroleum, machinery, transportation equipment |
| Highest Point: | 16,804 ft. (5,122 m) |
| Lowest Point: | Sea level |
| Area: | 300,948 sq. mi. (779,154 sq km) |

*ABOVE: Fine hand-woven carpets are an ancient Turkish tradition.*

*LEFT: Turkish flags surround a monument to national hero General Kemal Ataturk.*

# CYPRUS

The Kingdom of Cyprus was founded in 1193 and since that time, Cyprus has had an extremely conflict-laden history. After three hundred years as part of the Ottoman Empire (1571–1878), Cyprus was ruled by Britain until 1960. Upon gaining independence that year, Cyprus purposefully chose a flag with peaceful and neutral symbols. Upon the white field (which symbolizes peace and neutrality) is a map of the island. Although the map sometimes is depicted in copper to match the country's name, which means "Isle of Copper," it is often yellow.

Below the map of the island are two joined olive branches. The olive branches are a symbol of peace that dates back to the story of Noah in the Bible.

As a result of hostilities between the Turkish and Greek inhabitants on the island, Northern Cyprus has set up a separate government with a separate flag. This flag depicts a crescent moon and five-pointed star, which symbolizes the country's connection to Turkey, the only country which recognizes Northern Cyprus as a separate entity.

| | CYPRUS |
|---|---|
| Official Name: | Republic of Cyprus |
| Capital: | Nicosia |
| Languages: | Greek, Turkish |
| Religions: | Greek Orthodox, Muslim |
| Exports: | Food and beverages, clothing, cement |
| Imports: | Petroleum, machinery, transportation equipment, manufactured goods |
| Highest Point: | 6,401 ft. (1,951 m) |
| Lowest Point: | Sea level |
| Area: | 3,572 sq. mi. (9,248 sq km) |

# SYRIA

Syria was liberated in 1918 as a result of the Arab Revolt. Syria proclaimed independence in 1920 under a similar flag but was soon occupied by the French. Later a green and white flag, with the French Tricolor in the canton, was used. Before Syria became a republic in 1932, it adopted a green, white, and black flag with three red stars.

This particular flag remained in use after Syria's independence from France in 1946 and until Syria united with Egypt to form the United Arab Republic (UAR) in 1958. At this time, Syria adopted the same flag as Egypt (see **Egypt**). However, when Syria seceded from the UAR in 1961, it readopted its old flag. But in 1963, when Syria again proposed uniting with Egypt, as did Iraq, it altered its flag to duplicate that of Egypt, but with three green stars in the center, which represented the Arab revolution. In 1972, Syria became a member of the Federation of Arab Republics and replaced the star with a golden hawk. Since March 1980, Syria has flown the pan-Arab tricolor, the 1958 flag.

| | SYRIA |
|---|---|
| Official Name: | Syrian Arab Republic |
| Capital: | Damascus |
| Languages: | Arabic |
| Religions: | Sunni Muslim, Muslim, Christian |
| Exports: | Petroleum, textiles, cotton, fruit |
| Imports: | Machinery, fuels, metal products, food |
| Highest Point: | 9,232 ft. (2,814 m) |
| Lowest Point: | -655 ft. (-200 m) |
| Area: | 71,498 sq. mi. (185,108 sq km) |

*These Roman ruins are in Syria.*

# LEBANON

Lebanon became fully independent from France in 1946. Due to the intense religious struggles between its peoples, this country uses the neutral symbol of the cedar of Lebanon on its flag. This symbol, which represents strength, immortality, and holiness, dates back to 1861, when it first appeared on a flag; the symbol was revived in 1920, when a local government was set up under French mandate. The Lebanese flag was the French Tricolor with a cedar tree in the middle until the country adopted its present flag (created in 1943) whose colors not only symbolize the two dominant religions (Islam and Christianity) of its people, but self-sacrifice (red) and peace (white).

| | LEBANON |
|---|---|
| Official Name: | Republic of Lebanon |
| Capital: | Beirut |
| Languages: | Arabic, French, English |
| Religions: | Christian, Muslim, Drusean |
| Exports: | Fruits, vegetables, textiles |
| Imports: | Metals, machinery, food |
| Highest Point: | 10,115 ft. (3,083 m) |
| Lowest Point: | Sea level |
| Area: | 4,015 sq. mi. (10,395 sq km) |

# ISRAEL

Israel was proclaimed a state in May 1948. Its national flag, adopted in October of the same year, is based upon the flag used by the Zionist movement since 1891. The flag is inspired by the *tallith*, or prayer shawl, which is white with a blue horizontal band near both its upper and lower edges. The flag's center bears the emblem of the Zionist movement, two interlaced equilateral triangles which form the *Magen David*, or Shield of David, which has been a recognized Jewish symbol for centuries.

| ISRAEL | |
|---|---|
| Official Name: | State of Israel |
| Capital: | Jerusalem |
| Languages: | Hebrew, Arabic, English |
| Religions: | Jewish, Muslim |
| Exports: | Polished diamonds, fruits, textiles |
| Imports: | Military equipment, rough diamonds, petroleum |
| Highest Point: | 3,963 ft. (1,208 m) |
| Lowest Point: | -1,312 ft. (-400 m) |
| Area: | 8,302 sq. mi. (21,494 sq km) |

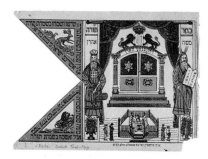

*RIGHT: Dome of the Rock, Jerusalem.*

*ABOVE: Simhath Torah flags.*

# JORDAN

Jordan has been an independent country since 1946. The Jordanian flag is a pan-Arab tricolor with a red triangle and a centered white, seven-pointed star at its hoist. The flag originated with King Hussein of the Hijaz in 1917. At that time, there was no star and the position of the green and white stripes was reversed. In 1920 his son, Emir Abdullah, occupied the area that is now Jordan and added the star to the flag to show that he considered his territory to be united with Syria. That flag was flown in Syria when that country was briefly ruled by his brother, King Feisal. The stripes were changed in 1922. In 1926, the region of Hejaz was annexed into Saudi Arabia, although King Hussein's two sons continued to fly the flag over Jordan and Iraq.

The star symbolizes the seven articles of Islamic belief. The colors of the flag are interpreted in many ways. One popular interpretation is that each color represents one of the ancient Caliphate families: black for the Abbasids; white, the Umayyads; green, the Fatimids; and red, the Hashemites, the family to which King Hussein belongs. Jordan is the only remaining part of the former Hashemite Empire.

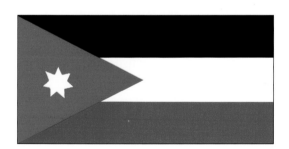

| JORDAN | |
|---|---|
| Official Name: | Hashemite Kingdom of Jordan |
| Capital: | Amman |
| Languages: | Arabic, English |
| Religions: | Sunni Muslim, Christian |
| Exports: | Phosphates, fruits, vegetables |
| Imports: | Machinery, transportation equipment, petroleum |
| Highest Point: | 5,755 ft. (1,754 m) |
| Lowest Point: | -1,312 ft. (-400 m) |
| Area: | 35,135 sq. mi. (90,965 sq km) |

# IRAQ

Iraq has been an independent country since 1932, although it used the same national flag from 1924 to 1959. During this time, Iraq's flag resembled the flag of its adjoining neighbor, Jordan, but had a trapezium in its hoist instead of a triangle, and two stars instead of one. A year after the overthrow of the monarchy in 1958, the flag's pattern was changed to a simplified version of the new national arms, which were based on the emblem of Shamash, the Babylonian sun god. This new flag had vertical stripes of black, white, and green with a large eight-pointed star. In 1963, the Arab Liberation Flag of red-white-black stripes was adopted by Iraq. There were three green stars at that time, but in 1991 the inscription "God Is Almighty" was added to the design by President Saddam Hussein.

| IRAQ | |
|---|---|
| Official Name: | Republic of Iraq |
| Capital: | Baghdad |
| Languages: | Arabic, Kurdish |
| Religions: | Shiite Muslim, Sunni Muslim, Christian |
| Exports: | Petroleum, dates |
| Imports: | Construction equipment, machinery, motor vehicles |
| Highest Point: | 11,835 ft. (3,607 m) |
| Lowest Point: | Sea level |
| Area: | 167,925 sq. mi. (434,758 sq km) |

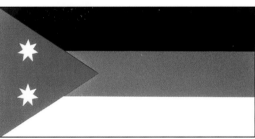

IRAQ; NATIONAL FLAG 1920–1921

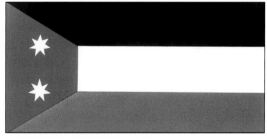

KINGDOM OF IRAQ; NATIONAL FLAG 1924–1959

REPUBLIC OF IRAQ; NATIONAL FLAG 1959–1963

## SAUDI ARABIA

Arabia was first united by Muhammad in the early seventh century. His successors conquered the entire Middle East and North Africa, bringing with them Islam and the Arabic language. During this time many different flags were used, mostly red or green. Later, in the mid-eighteenth century, the Pure Islam movement adopted the green flag of Muhammad, the prophet, or messenger, of Allah. The color green was said to be the favorite color of Muhammad and to symbolize, to the Arab peoples of the desert, paradise. This flag was taken up by Ibn Saud, the founder of the Saudi family, who overthrew the Turks and went on to dominate the region. (Early Saudi flags also had a white vertical stripe at the hoist.)

The Saudis added the *shahada,* the Moslem statement of faith, in white letters. The sword of Abdul Aziz (a symbolic sword given to him by his father), who conquered the independent state of Nejd in 1906 and, later, other parts of Arabia, was soon added as well. Perhaps because the sword was symbolic, it appeared in many ways through the years, sometimes even as two crossed swords. In 1973, the sword as it now appears was standardized. The inscription, which translated means "There is no God but Allah and Muhammad is the Prophet [read "messenger"] of Allah," by law must be able to be read correctly (from right to left) from both sides of the flag.

| SAUDI ARABIA | |
|---|---|
| Official Name: | Kingdom of Saudi Arabia |
| Capital: | Riyadh |
| Languages: | Arabic |
| Religions: | Muslim |
| Exports: | Petroleum, petroleum products |
| Imports: | Manufactured goods, transportation equipment, construction materials |
| Highest Point: | 10,279 ft. (3,133 m) |
| Lowest Point: | Sea level |
| Area: | 830,000 sq. mi. (2,148,870 sq km) |

*Mosques (here in Saudi Arabia) are the center of Islamic religious life.*

## YEMEN

Yemen was divided into the separate countries of North Yemen and South Yemen until April 1990.

The area once called North Yemen was under Turkish domination for many years, until 1918, when it became an independent country. From 1927 to August 1962, the country flew a red flag with a white sword and five white stars. The red field symbolized the Shia sect of Islam, and the stars represented either the five relatives of the Prophet, deeply respected by the Shiites, or the five basic duties of Islam: fasting, prayer, alms, pilgrimage to Mecca (the holy city of Islam), and belief in the one God, Allah.

In September 1962, Imam Ahmed (who had ruled from 1948) was assassinated by revolutionaries who desired a republican regime and drew their inspiration from the Egyptian leader, Gamal Abdel Nasser. These forces, therefore, flew the Arab liberation colors. A civil war raged until 1970, and during this period of strife, each faction flew their respective colors. The revolutionary forces won out, and the Arab Liberation Flag with a single green five-pointed star in the center, used by the revolutionary forces, thereafter was the sole national flag of Yemen.

The area of Yemen that was formerly South Yemen before unification was once South Arabia and Aden, which has been a port of trade for incense, spice, and silk between the East and West for at least two thousand years. In 1839, Britain seized control of the region, which provided the English with a controlling position at the

Red Sea's southern entrance. In 1959, the British attempted to form, with local dynastic rulers, the Federation of South Arabia, which included Aden; but in 1963, a war of independence began, waged by the National Liberation Front (NLF), and the Egypt-supported Front for the Liberation of Occupied South Yemen. In 1967, the NLF won and independence was achieved. The flag of South Yemen was modeled after the Egyptian flag. The blue triangle at the hoist represented the Yemeni people; the red star in the triangle represented the NLF, which was the ruling party of South Yemen until the country was peacefully joined with North Yemen in 1990.

The current flag of Yemen is a red, white, and black tricolor with no adornment.

| YEMEN | |
|---|---|
| Official Name: | Republic of Yemen |
| Capital: | Sanaa |
| Languages: | Arabic |
| Religions: | Muslim |
| Exports: | Petroleum products, fish products, hides, khat, cotton, coffee |
| Imports: | Manufactured goods, petroleum products, textiles, food, machinery, petroleum, transportation equipment |
| Highest Point: | 12,336 ft. (3,760 m) |
| Lowest Point: | Sea level |
| Area: | 193,125 sq. mi. (500,000 sq km) |

# OMAN

Oman utilized a red flag that represented its identification with an ancient Islamic sect, the Kharidjites, who, from at least the 1600s until modern times, commonly flew a red flag along the Arabian shores of the Persian Gulf and their Indian Ocean–based colonies. In 1970, Sultan Said bin Taimur was overthrown by his son, the present sultan, who changed the country's name to the Sultanate of Oman and introduced a new national flag that utilizes the traditional emblem of the ruling Sa'idi dynasty, a belt with a dagger superimposed on a pair of crossed swords. This emblem, slightly altered in 1985, was placed in the flag's canton; panels of white and green were added to the fly. The green is said to symbolize the green mountains of the region.

| OMAN | |
|---|---|
| Official Name: | Sultanate of Oman |
| Capital: | Muscat |
| Languages: | Arabic, Farsi |
| Religions: | Ibadite Muslim, Sunni Muslim, Shiite Muslim |
| Exports: | Petroleum |
| Imports: | Machinery, transportation equipment, manufactured goods, food |
| Highest Point: | 9,957 ft. (3,035 m) |
| Lowest Point: | Sea level |
| Area: | 82,030 sq. mi. (212,376 sq km) |

# UNITED ARAB EMIRATES

In 1820, many small Arab states along the southern coast of the Persian Gulf signed the "General Treaty" with Britain, agreeing to add some white into their completely red flags as a symbol that they would henceforth be at peace with each other and the British. Six of the signatory states—Abu Dhabi, Ajman, Dubai, Ras al-Khaimah, Sharjah, and Umm al-Qaiwain—formed the Trucial States Council in 1966 together with Fujairah, which had never signed the General Treaty and therefore used a plain red flag. The flag of the Council was white with red borders at the top and bottom and a seven-pointed green star in the center. Five years later, the states federated, gaining recognition from Great Britain as the independent United Arab Emirates. At this time, the present flag was adopted in the pan-Arab colors. The red vertical stripe at the hoist is a reminder that red is the basic flag color of the seven emirates.

| UNITED ARAB EMIRATES | |
|---|---|
| Official Name: | United Arab Emirates |
| Capital: | Abu Dhabi |
| Languages: | Arabic, Farsi, English |
| Religions: | Muslim |
| Exports: | Petroleum |
| Imports: | Machinery, consumer goods, food |
| Highest Point: | 3,200 ft. (975 m) |
| Lowest Point: | Sea level |
| Area: | 32,278 sq. mi. (83,568 sq km) |

# BAHRAIN

Bahrain is a very old coastal state that, in 1783, was freed from Persian dominance by the present-day dynasty. Like other Persian Gulf states controlled by the Kharidjites, Bahrain flew a plain red flag until the General Treaty with Britain in 1820 (see **United Arab Emirates**). At the time of the treaty, Bahrain adopted a plain white vertical band; in 1932, the state serrated the dividing line, possibly to make the flag unique among the other emirates. Bahrain achieved final independence from Britain in 1971.

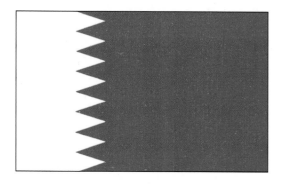

| BAHRAIN | |
|---|---|
| Official Name: | State of Bahrain |
| Capital: | Manama |
| Languages: | Arabic, English |
| Religions: | Shiite Muslim, Sunni Muslim |
| Exports: | Petroleum, aluminum, fish |
| Imports: | Machinery, motor vehicles, manufactured goods, food |
| Highest Point: | 440 ft. (134 m) |
| Lowest Point: | Sea level |
| Area: | 256 sq. mi. (663 sq km) |

# QATAR

Qatar was once subject to Bahrain, and therefore once flew a plain red flag (see **Bahrain**). In 1860, a white serrated band was added along the flag's hoist. The flag differs in width from other flags in the region and has a unique color. On earlier flags, Qatar's name appeared in white letters, and red diamonds were placed on the white section. In 1949, the plain flag came

into use, and the color was altered from red to a maroon. This color is based on the way in which red pigment made from local vegetable dyes reacts to the sun. The color and shape are official.

| QATAR | |
|---|---|
| Official Name: | State of Qatar |
| Capital: | Doha |
| Languages: | Arabic, English |
| Religions: | Muslim |
| Exports: | Petroleum |
| Imports: | Machinery, transportation equipment, manufactured goods, food |
| Highest Point: | 344 ft. (105 m) |
| Lowest Point: | Sea level |
| Area: | 4,247 sq. mi. (10,995 sq km) |

# KUWAIT

Kuwait, like many other Arab regions, flew a plain red flag to show its allegiance to the Ottoman Empire. In 1899, however, Kuwait became a British protectorate and added to the flag's hoist a white stripe and the name of the state in white. When Kuwait became independent from Britain in 1961, it created a flag in pan-Arab colors. The official interpretation of the colors is as follows: black represents Kuwait's battlefields; green, its pastures; white, its deeds; and red, dyed with the blood of the enemy, is its future.

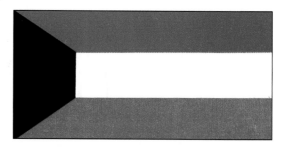

| KUWAIT | |
|---|---|
| Official Name: | State of Kuwait |
| Capital: | Kuwait |
| Languages: | Arabic, English |
| Religions: | Muslim |
| Exports: | Petroleum and petroleum products |
| Imports: | Machinery, transportation equipment, manufactured goods, fuels |
| Highest Point: | 951 ft. (290 m) |
| Lowest Point: | Sea level |
| Area: | 6,880 sq. mi. (17,812 sq km) |

# IRAN

Iran is an ancient kingdom that has been independent since the beginning of the sixteenth century. Since the eighteenth century, red, white, and green flags have been used in Iran, although there is no consensus about what the colors signify. In the nineteenth century, Iran began to use flags that included the emblem of a lion standing in front of a rising sun and holding the sword of Ali. The son-in-law of Muhammad, Ali is a deeply respected figure in the Shia sect, which is mostly based in Iran. Use of the lion and sun emblem in Iran is much older than the sword, however. This emblem was used with several other flag designs until the shah of Iran was ousted from power in 1979, after which it was removed. A year after the Ayatollah Khomeini returned to Iran in 1979 and assumed power, the present design with the Arabic symbol was adopted. The Arabic inscription reads *Allahu Akbar* ("God is great") and occurs twenty-two times, signifying the date of the Ayatollah's return — 22 Bahman 1357 (February 11, 1979).

| IRAN | |
|---|---|
| Official Name: | Islamic Republic of Iran |
| Capital: | Teheran |
| Languages: | Farsi, Turkish, Kurdish, Arabic |
| Religions: | Shiite Muslim, Sunni Muslim, Zoroastrian, Jewish |
| Exports: | Petroleum, carpets, fruits, nuts |
| Imports: | Machinery, military equipment, food |
| Highest Point: | 18,386 ft. (5,604 m) |
| Lowest Point: | -92 ft. (-28 m) |
| Area: | 636,296 sq. mi. (1,647,370 sq km) |

## AFGHANISTAN

When Britain recognized the independence of Afghanistan in 1919, the national flag of the latter was black with a white emblem in the center. King Amanullah introduced a new flag in 1928 as part of his modernization program, but this black-red-green horizontal tricolor disappeared when he was overthrown by conservatives. The old flag was restored, but the following year a modified version of the tricolor was

adopted by King Nadir Shah. He made it acceptable to traditionalists by putting a religious symbol in the center. Variations of the black-red-green have been used ever since that time, except during the extreme Marxist regime of 1978–1980. In 1974, the mosque, an Islamic device, was altered and replaced by a combined pulpit and niche, which symbolize the mosque (the niche shows the direction of Mecca). From 1980 through 1987, when Soviet troops attempted to control the country, the Koran and a red star appeared on the emblem. In the past, several emblems carried the name of the country and the date of the current constitution, but since 1980 the scroll has had no inscription.

| AFGHANISTAN | |
|---|---|
| Official Name: | Republic of Afghanistan |
| Capital: | Kabul |
| Languages: | Dari, Pushtu |
| Religions: | Sunni Muslim, Shiite Muslim |
| Exports: | Fruits, nuts, natural gas, carpets |
| Imports: | Food, petroleum |
| Highest Point: | 24,557 ft. (7,485 m) |
| Lowest Point: | 837 ft. (255 m) |
| Area: | 250,000 sq. mi. (647,250 sq km) |

*The lakes at Band-i-Amir in Afghanistan.*

## PAKISTAN

Pakistan became independent in 1947, led by the Moslem League, an Indian nationalist movement that, since 1906, used a solid green flag with the crescent and star of Islam. Upon independence, the white stripe was added and was initially said to represent the non-Moslem minorities of the nation: the Buddhists, Hindus, Christians, and others. As of 1964, the official interpretation of the flag has been as follows: green represents prosperity; white, peace; the crescent, progress; and the star, enlightenment.

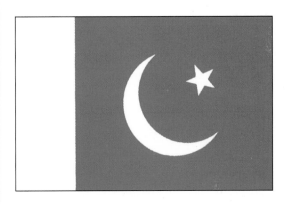

| PAKISTAN | |
|---|---|
| Official Name: | Islamic Republic of Pakistan |
| Capital: | Islamabad |
| Languages: | Urdu, English, Panjabi, Baluchi |
| Religions: | Muslim |
| Exports: | Rice, cotton, textiles, light manufactured goods |
| Imports: | Petroleum, transportation equipment, raw materials |
| Highest Point: | 28,250 ft. (8,611 m) |
| Lowest Point: | Sea level |
| Area: | 339,732 sq. mi. (879,566 sq km) |

*The Taj Mahal is recognized as one of the world's greatest architectural achievements.*

# INDIA

India's national flag is one of the first flags to be derived from a political party flag. The flag of Mahatma Gandhi's party, the Indian National Congress, was originally white, green, and red; in 1933, it was altered to orange, white, and green, with an emblem of a blue stylized spinning wheel in the center. The spinning wheel symbolized Gandhi's self-sufficiency program for India, then under British domination. At independence, Indians replaced the spinning-wheel image with the image of peaceful change, the Chakra (wheel) of Asoka, the Buddhist king. The symbol of the Chakra has great importance in Indian culture, for it symbolizes the inevitability of existence. The twenty-four spokes of the wheel represent the number of hours in the day. The color orange is interpreted as symbolizing sacrifice and courage; white, truth and peace; and green, fertility and faith.

In India, law stipulates that private citizens fly the flag only on specific national festivals.

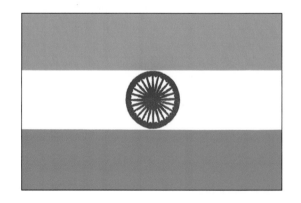

## MALDIVES

The Maldive Islands, which translated literally means "the state of the thousand islands," in earlier times flew a plain red flag, common among many coastal Islamic states (see **Oman** and **United Arab Emirates**). The Maldives continued to fly a red flag even after becoming a British protectorate in the late 1880s. To distinguish its national flag from similar ones in neighboring countries, an early twentieth-century prime minister added a green central rectangle with a white crescent. Other variations of that design were used by the military, the ruling sultan, and merchant ships. Until the Maldives' independence in 1965, the flag also had a border of black and white stripes at the hoist.

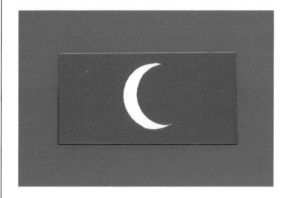

## SRI LANKA

Sri Lanka, called Ceylon until 1972, was held by the British from 1796 until 1948, when the country became an independent nation within the Commonwealth. The main section of the national flag is taken from the Buddhist Sinhalese (who make up most of the inhabitants) royal flag, which belonged to the last king of Kandy, the last state on the island to come under British domination. (This flag was a different shade of red with a gold border and the golden lion in the center grasping a sword.) In 1948, upon the country's independence, the objects in the corners were ancient Ceylonese pinnacles; however, in 1972, the leaves from the *bo*, or *pipul*, tree, which is closely associated with Buddha, replaced the pinnacles. In 1951, orange and green panels were added to the flag to represent the Hindu and Moslem minorities.

**INDIA**

| | |
|---|---|
| Official Name: | Republic of India |
| Capital: | New Delhi |
| Languages: | Hindi, English, indigenous |
| Religions: | Hindu, Muslim, Christian, Sikh |
| Exports: | Engineering goods, textiles, clothing |
| Imports: | Machinery, transportation equipment, petroleum |
| Highest Point: | 28,208 ft. (8,598 m) |
| Lowest Point: | Sea level |
| Area: | 1,237,061 sq. mi. (3,202,751 sq km) |

**MALDIVES**

| | |
|---|---|
| Official Name: | Republic of Maldives |
| Capital: | Male |
| Languages: | Divehi |
| Religions: | Sunni Muslim |
| Exports: | Fish products, clothing |
| Imports: | Food, manufactured goods, machinery, petroleum |
| Highest Point: | 80 ft. (24 m) |
| Lowest Point: | Sea level |
| Area: | 115 sq. mi. (298 sq km) |

**SRI LANKA**

| | |
|---|---|
| Official Name: | Democratic Socialist Republic of Sri Lanka |
| Capital: | Colombo |
| Languages: | Sinhala, Tamil, English |
| Religions: | Buddhist, Hindu, Christian, Muslim |
| Exports: | Tea, natural rubber, petroleum, textiles |
| Imports: | Petroleum, machinery, transportation equipment, sugar |
| Highest Point: | 8,281 ft. (2,524 m) |
| Lowest Point: | Sea level |
| Area: | 24,962 sq. mi. (64,627 sq km) |

TOP: *The famous Palace of the Winds, Jaipur, India.* BOTTOM: *A goddess in Mysore, India, plays the sitar.*

## NEPAL

Nepal was united into one kingdom in 1768 and has been an independent nation since that time. While no one is certain of the origins of this unique flag, it is known that, similar to the flag of Ethiopia, it began as two red, right-angled triangular pennants, each with a blue border, that were flown one above the other. The upper triangle carries the moon emblem of the royal family, while the lower triangle carries the sun emblem of the Ráná family, the hereditary prime ministerial family, which exercised supreme power in Nepal until 1951. Nepal's flag, the only national flag not rectangular in shape, is said to be the embodiment of a prayer that Nepal may flourish so long as the sun and moon exist.

| NEPAL | |
|---|---|
| Official Name: | Kingdom of Nepal |
| Capital: | Kathmandu |
| Languages: | Nepali |
| Religions: | Hindu, Buddhist |
| Exports: | Rice, food, jute, wood |
| Imports: | Consumer goods, fuels, machinery |
| Highest Point: | 29,028 ft. (8,848 m) |
| Lowest Point: | 197 ft. (60 m) |
| Area: | 56,135 sq. mi. (145,333 sq km) |

*In 1953 Great Britain's Sir Edmund Hillary was the first to plant a flag on the top of Nepal's Mount Everest.*

## BHUTAN

In Bhutan during the thirteenth century, Tsangha Gyarey Yeshey Dori erected a monastery and named it the Druk (the "Thunder Dragon"—in Bhutan, thunder is believed to be the voice of dragons); con-

sequently, Dori's followers were known as Drukpas. Since that time, the name and the emblem of the dragon has been associated with Bhutan. While the flag's background colors have changed over the years, its orange triangle represents the Drukpa monasteries, while the yellowish triangle stands for the Wangchuks, the royal dynasty. Bhutan's independence was recognized by India in 1949, and it became a constitutional monarchy in 1969.

© Steve Vidler/Leo de Wys, Inc.

| | BHUTAN |
|---|---|
| Official Name: | Kingdom of Bhutan |
| Capital: | Thimbu |
| Languages: | Dzongkha, English, Nepalese dialects |
| Religions: | Buddhist, Hindu |
| Exports: | Agricultural products, wood, coal |
| Imports: | Textiles, grain, motor vehicles, fuels |
| Highest Point: | 24,748 ft. (7,543 m) |
| Lowest Point: | 318 ft. (97 m) |
| Area: | 18,147 sq. mi. (46,982 sq km) |

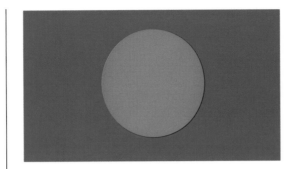

| | BANGLADESH |
|---|---|
| Official Name: | People's Republic of Bangladesh |
| Capital: | Dacca |
| Languages: | English, Bengali |
| Religions: | Muslim, Hindu |
| Exports: | Jute, leather, tea |
| Imports: | Grain, fuels, cotton, fertilizer |
| Highest Point: | 3,141 ft. (957 m) |
| Lowest Point: | Sea level |
| Area: | 55,598 sq. mi. (143,943 sq km) |

*Elaborate temples are characteristic of the architecture of Myanmar.*

# BANGLADESH

Bangladesh was under British domination from the mid-eighteenth century until 1947, when East Bengal became part of Pakistan. The Awami League, based in the east, charging West Pakistani domination, won control of the National Assembly in 1971. When riots broke out, Pakistani troops attacked on March 25, 1971, and the next day Bangladesh declared its independence. The flag under which the independence struggle occurred resembled the present flag except that it had a yellow silhouette of a map of Bangladesh in the red disk. This was supposed to stand for the concept of the "Golden Bengal" of the national anthem. To facilitate manufacturing the flag, the map was struck when the flag was officially adopted in 1972. The color green represents the fruitful land. The red disk symbolizes freedom.

# MYANMAR

The Union of Myanmar, formerly Burma, won its independence in 1948, after nearly a century of British rule. Myanmar's national flag was introduced at that time. The emblem in the canton changed; it originally contained a large white star surrounded by five smaller stars. The large star in this emblem was derived from the Anti-Fascist Resistance Movement during World War II. The five smaller stars represented the five ethnic groups in the country: Burmese, Chin, Kachin, Karen, and Shan. In 1974, the new constitution created the new emblem in which the fourteen stars represent the seven states and seven divisions of the nation.

| | MYANMAR |
|---|---|
| Official Name: | Union of Myanmar |
| Capital: | Yankon |
| Languages: | Burmese, indigenous |
| Religions: | Buddhist, animistic, Christian, others |
| Exports: | Rice, teak, hardwoods, base metals |
| Imports: | Machinery, transportation equipment, construction materials |
| Highest Point: | 19,296 ft. (5,881 m) |
| Lowest Point: | Sea level |
| Area: | 261,228 sq. mi. (676,319 sq km) |

*Statues of demons decorate the Golden Temple Wat Phra Kao in Bangkok, Thailand.*

# THAILAND

Thailand, once called Siam, has been a kingdom since the Middle Ages. Called the "Land of the White Elephant" in legend, Thailand placed a white elephant on its flag from 1817 to 1916. Before 1817, the flag was red and bore the image of the Chakra, a wheel with flamelike blades emerging from its rim. This wheel is related to the Chakra used on the flag of India (see **India**). After 1855, the wheel was removed and the white elephant, a symbol of the ancient Thai kings, was substituted. In 1892, the elephant was depicted with harness and ornaments; on the government flag, the animal was shown standing on a pedestal. In 1916, a civil ensign, of red with two white stripes, was introduced. In 1917, the center stripe was made blue to express Thailand's solidarity with the Allies in World War II. Thailand's flag, since that time, has come to be known as the *Trairanga,* or the Tricolor. Although the white elephant is no longer on the flag, it is still considered to be a holy animal.

|  | THAILAND |
|---|---|
| Official Name: | Kingdom of Thailand |
| Capital; | Bangkok |
| Languages: | Thai |
| Religions: | Buddhist, Muslim |
| Exports: | Rice, natural rubber, sugar, tapioca |
| Imports: | Machinery, transportation equipment, petroleum |
| Highest Point: | 8,530 ft. (2,600 m) |
| Lowest Point: | Sea level |
| Area: | 198,115 sq. mi. (512,920 sq km) |

# VIETNAM

Vietnam, once divided into North and South, now uses the flag of North Vietnam. Ho Chi Minh and his followers were the first to use the red flag and star, symbols derived from communist China, when they established a republic in Hanoi in 1945. At that time, the star was of obtuse design; it is now five-pointed.

South Vietnam's flag was a yellow field with three red horizontal stripes and dated back to 1948. In 1960, the National Liberation Front (whose flag was red over blue with a centered yellow star) sought control over the reigning regime and, in 1975, was victorious. South Vietnam collapsed that year.

In 1976, North Vietnam took over South Vietnam to become one socialist republic, Vietnam, whose flag remains, to this day, the flag of the North. The red color represents the revolution. The five-pointed star is the universal emblem of communist countries and symbolizes the five areas of the population: peasants, workers, youth, soldiers, and intellectuals.

|  | VIETNAM |
|---|---|
| Official Name: | Socialist Republic of Vietnam |
| Capital: | Hanoi |
| Languages: | Vietnamese |
| Religions: | Buddhist, Confucian, Taoist, Roman Catholic |
| Exports: | Agricultural products, handicrafts, coal |
| Imports: | Petroleum, steel products, railroad equipment |
| Highest Point: | 10,312 ft. (3,143 m) |
| Lowest Point: | Sea level |
| Area: | 127,242 sq. mi. (329,430 sq km) |

# CAMBODIA

Cambodia, formerly Kampuchea, has been, in one form or another, an independent state since 1953. At the present time, there are several rival factions vying for control of the government; yet these factions fly similar flags, which depict different silhouetted versions of the temple in the ruined city of Angkor Wat, which dates back to approximately A.D. 1100. The temple of Angkor Wat originally appeared on a flag in the nineteenth century. In 1948, the flag portrayed a detailed temple in white against a red field with wide blue borders and was used until 1970, when pro–United States premier Lon Nol seized power. At this time, the flag's field was changed to blue with the temple on a red canton and three white stars on the upper fly. In 1976, after the Khmer Rouge forces captured Phnom Penh, the flag was altered again to depict a three-tower temple. A new government, supported by the Vietnamese, established a five-towered temple flag in 1979. Both regimes changed their flags again in 1989–1990. Finally, in 1991 the present design was created for the ruling Supreme National Council. It shows the light blue and white colors of the United Nations as a neutral background for a flag displaying a map and the name of the country.

| CAMBODIA | |
|---|---|
| Official Name: | Cambodia |
| Capital: | Phnom Penh |
| Languages: | Khmer |
| Religions: | Theravada Buddhist |
| Exports: | Natural rubber |
| Imports: | Food, machinery, petroleum |
| Highest Point: | 5,810 ft. (1,771 m) |
| Lowest Point: | Sea level |
| Area: | 69,898 sq. mi. |
| | (180,966 sq km) |

*The temple of Angkor Wat was featured on the flag of Cambodia for decades. Seven centuries ago thousands of workmen struggled to build the great temple.*

# LAOS

Laos became fully independent of French rule in 1953, although its first flag, used until 1953, dates back to the nineteenth century. This original flag was red, with a three-headed white elephant under an umbrella; this emblem not only symbolized the ancient name of the nation, "Land of a Million Elephants," but also represented the unification of three regions under a single dynasty. However, in 1953, the royal government and the Pathet Lao, whose flag was blue with a red border at the top and bottom and a white disk in the center, entered a civil war. During 1973 and 1974, the Pathet Lao and the monarchy formed a coalition government, but in 1975 the Pathet Lao assumed complete power, declared a people's republic, and forced the king to abdicate. The Pathet Lao flag became the new national flag at that time. The colors are interpreted as follows: red stands for the blood shed in the fight for freedom; blue, modern prosperity; the white disk, a bright future.

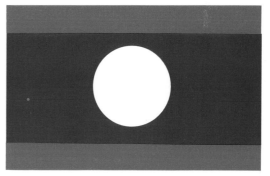

| LAOS | |
|---|---|
| Official Name: | Lao People's Democratic Republic |
| Capital: | Vientiane |
| Languages: | Lao, French |
| Religions: | Buddhist, animistic, others |
| Exports: | Hydroelectric power, wood, coffee, tin |
| Imports: | Food, petroleum, machinery, transportation equipment |
| Highest Point: | 9,252 ft. (2,820 m) |
| Lowest Point: | 230 ft. (70 m) |
| Area: | 91,429 sq. mi. (236,710 sq km) |

© Smith/Envision

# THE PEOPLE'S REPUBLIC OF CHINA

Proclaimed the People's Republic of China in 1949, China is an ancient country with a deep and rich flag history. China's first national flag was adopted in 1872. This flag was yellow and bore the emblem of a blue dragon; the color blue and the dragon are the symbols of the East, which the Chinese viewed as the center of the world (symbolized by the color yellow). Yellow was also the color of the Manchu dynasty, which ruled the country for many years. When parts of the army revolted in 1911, the flag design was changed, and became five stripes—red, yellow, blue, white, and black.

During the 1920s, many Soviet republics were set up; each adopted a red flag like its Soviet parent. In 1928, the Red Army was formed: This organization used a red flag that carried the Chinese characters for one and eight (representing August 1) as well as a stylized yellow star, which differed from the hollow star that adorned the Soviet Union's flag. (This flag is still the flag of the People's Liberation Army.) That same year the recognized government of China adopted a new national flag. It consisted of a red field with the party flag of the Kuo Min Tang (a white sun on a dark blue field) in the upper hoist corner. Still in use today on the island of Taiwan, this flag was used in China until the military defeat of the Nationalist forces in 1949, when the present flag of the People's Republic took its place.

The large star of China's present flag is three times the size of the four smaller ones, and the flag is always in a 2:3 proportion. The placement of each star on the flag is specified exactly. The large star represents communism, while the four smaller ones symbolize the four social classes of the republic: peasants, workers, petty bourgeoisie, and patriotic capitalists. The red field symbolizes revolution, but it also echoes the color of the Han dynasty, 206 B.C.–A.D. 220.

| THE PEOPLE'S REPUBLIC OF CHINA | |
|---|---|
| Official Name: | People's Republic of China |
| Capital: | Beijing |
| Languages: | Chinese dialects |
| Religions: | Confucian, Taoist, Buddhist |
| Exports: | Manufactured goods, agricultural products, petroleum |
| Imports: | Grain, chemical fertilizer, raw materials |
| Highest Point: | 29,028 ft. (8,848 m) |
| Lowest Point: | -505 ft. (-154 m) |
| Area: | 3,718,783 sq. mi. (9,627,929 sq km) |

© Fridmar Damm/Leo de Wys, Inc.

ABOVE: *The Ming emperors had huge stone statues created to decorate their mausoleums.*

BELOW: *The Chinese national flag is displayed in Tiananmen Square, site of the 1989 massacre of students.*

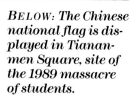

© James Simon/New England Stock Photo

*EMPIRE OF CHINA; WAR ENSIGN 1890-1912*

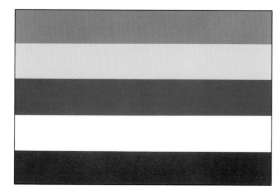

*REPUBLIC OF CHINA; NATIONAL FLAG 1912-1928*

*TIBET; NATIONAL FLAG C. 1912-C. 1959*

*ABOVE, RIGHT: The Great Wall was originally built to keep Mongols away from the cities of China.*

*RIGHT: The dragon was featured on Chinese flags prior to 1912, when the empire was overthrown.*

## *MONGOLIA*

Mongolia gained final independence from China in 1921 and, in 1924, was the first country outside the Soviet Union to have a communist government. Its first flag was, therefore, red and in its center was a blue (blue is the color of the Mongol race and represents the sky) *soyonbo*, the traditional emblem of the country. The symbols of the mystical *soyonbo* represent the following, from bottom to top: the triangle symbolizes fire; the square, the earth; the yin-yang (see **South Korea**), water; the crescent moon, the sun, air, and the flame represent ether, the upper regions of space. The emblem as a whole resembles the ritual dagger used by the holy lamas to cast out devils. This first flag of Mongolia, which was used until 1940, also included a stylized lotus emblem at the bottom of the *soyonbo*. The communist star, which appeared over the *soyonbo* in the flag, was removed by the new constitution of 1992. While the color red symbolizes the revolution, it also represents love and victory. The color yellow represents eternal friendship.

| MONGOLIA | |
|---|---|
| Official Name: | Mongolia |
| Capital: | Ulan Bator |
| Languages: | Khalkha Mongolian |
| Religions: | Tibetan Buddhist, Muslim |
| Exports: | Livestock, animal products, wool, hides |
| Imports: | Machinery, petroleum, clothing, materials |
| Highest Point: | 14,350 ft. (4,373 m) |
| Lowest Point: | 1,814 ft. (553 m) |
| Area: | 604,250 sq. mi. (1,564,403 sq km) |

*Soviet tanks guarding the Russian Federation headquarters, August 20, 1991.*

## *COMMONWEALTH OF INDEPENDENT STATES*
### *(Formerly The Soviet Union)*

Prior to the Bolshevik Revolution of 1917, the person who exercised the greatest influence upon the flags of Russia was the czar Peter the Great, the monarch who reigned from 1682 to 1725 and created the Russian navy. In 1699, Peter the Great, using a design taken from the flag of the Netherlands, created the white, blue, and red tricolor of Imperial Russia. This tricolor flag became the basic national flag and civil ensign as well as the inspiration for the pan-Slavic colors. The pan-Slavic colors were adopted by Serbia, Slovakia, Croatia, Bosnia, and other Slavic lands dominated by foreign rule.

The Imperial naval ensign was white with a blue saltire and honored St. Andrew, the patron saint of Russia. The Imperial standard was a yellow flag with the arms of the czar in the center. There were two forms of this flag (one for use on land, one for use at sea), which bore the two-headed eagle (inherited from the Byzantine Empire) bearing the shields of the czar's territory. After March 1917, with the abdication of the czar, all royal flags and emblems were discontinued. The tricolor and the two-headed eagle, without its crown, continued to be used by the Kerensky regime until it was toppled in November of that year.

After Kerensky's fall, there was much change: Civil war began, rival regimes were established, and several provinces declared independence. Ultimately, Estonia, Finland, Latvia, Lithuania, and Poland remained independent, but many other regions, including the Ukraine and Armenia eventually were made a part of the new Soviet state.

The red flag of the Bolshevik revolution was actually first used during the French Revolution, and signified the power of the people over autocratic rule, especially in the Paris Commune of 1871. The red flag first appeared in Russia during the 1905 uprising and resurfaced in 1917 as the flag of the left-wing parties. During this same period, the red star of communism also made its first appearance on the flag of the Red Army. During the revolution, red flags with inscriptions were often used, but as the new party became established, more traditional flags were introduced. In July 1918, the first Soviet Republic, Russia, adopted a red flag, with the gold initials of the republic in the canton. Variations of that flag were in use until 1954, although the Soviet Union was created in 1922, when it was given a distinctive flag of its own. To the revolutionary Red Banner were added the hammer and sickle, symbolizing the union of workers and peasants, and a five-pointed star, emblematic of the five continents which were eventually supposed to be under communist rule.

In 1991, the Union of Soviet Socialist Republics (USSR) contained fifteen union republics. While each republic could fly its own flag, by communist law it had to be based on the red flag and had to bear the hammer and sickle as well as the five-pointed star used as a badge by the Bolsheviks.

In August 1991, hard-line communist leaders attempted unsuccessfully to turn back recent gains made by the Soviet people under Mikhail S. Gorbachev. When this coup failed, the Soviet Union almost instantly plunged into a profound transformation that reshaped its very structure. The Communist party was ousted from power, and the party's apparatus was dismantled. Russia, the largest of the Union Republics, returned to using the white, blue, and red tricolor it used before the Revolution of 1917.

The other republics threw out the Union Treaty, completely slashing the powers that were previously centered in Moscow. A new agreement was drafted that recognized each member republic to be a sovereign state, with the right to establish direct diplomatic ties with other countries as well as to have sole control over their own land and resources. It also stated that each could del- egate certain powers to a central government. These powers might include control of the borders, command of a small armed force, and the right to issue a single currency. At the time of this writing, however, the only certainty is that the USSR has undergone a transformation as dramatic as the 1917 Revolution.

© Steve Vidler/Leo de Wys, Inc.

*St. Basil's Cathedral in Moscow is world famous.*

Many of the former republics of the Soviet Union adopted flags that they had used previously when independent, or variations of those flags. In Central Asia, however, the borders had been completely redrawn under communist rule; in any event, the independent states of the nineteenth century had had no national flags which could be revived. Consequently, at the time this book was written, several of the newly independent states were still using flags with the old Marxist-Leninist symbolism.

*SOVIET UNION: 1955–1991*

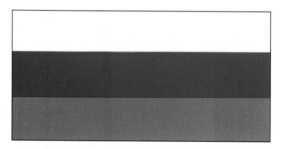

*RUSSIA; 1992*

| RUSSIA | |
|---|---|
| Official Name: | Russian Federation |
| Capital: | Moscow |
| Languages: | Russian |
| Religions: | Christianity |
| Exports: | Unavailable at this time |
| Imports: | Unavailable at this time |
| Highest Point: | 18,510 ft. (5,642 m) |
| Lowest Point: | -92 ft. (-28 m) |
| Area: | 6,593,391 sq. mi. (17,076,882 sq km) |

# BELARUS

The name of this country, formerly known as Byelorussia, means "White Russia." Its first flag was plain white, but this was quickly changed; the red stripe was added so that the flag would not look like a flag of surrender. The colors also appear in the national coat of arms, a white mounted knight on a red shield. That heraldry dates to the Middle Ages, while the flag was developed in 1917. Belarus lost its independence in 1919, but seventy years later the flag was revived. The flag was given legal recognition in 1991, following the proclamation of statehood.

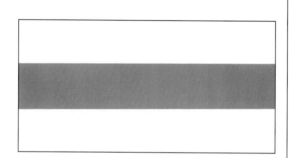

| BELARUS | |
|---|---|
| Official Name: | Republic of Belarus |
| Capital: | Minsk |
| Languages: | Belarussian |
| Religions: | Russian Orthodox, Roman Catholic, Baptist, Seventh Day Adventist, Judaism, Muslim |
| Exports: | Ferrous metals, pulp and paper, building materials and components |
| Imports: | Nonferrous metals, agricultural materials, oil, food |
| Highest Point: | 1,135 ft. (346 m) |
| Lowest Point: | 279 ft. (85 m) |
| Area: | 80,154 sq. mi. (207,599 sq km) |

# UKRAINE

In 1848, many Slavic nations rose in revolt against autocratic rulers. They adopted distinctive colors for flags; these were first used by ethnic groups and later by independent nations. Ukraine chose blue and yellow, said to stand for the sky and vast fields of grain for which the country is famous. First made official in 1918 when Ukraine proclaimed its independence, the blue-yellow flag was suppressed by the Communists after 1920, revived in 1989, and again made official two years later.

| UKRAINE | |
|---|---|
| Official Name: | Ukraine |
| Capital: | Kyiv |
| Languages: | Ukrainian, Russian |
| Religions: | Ukrainian Autocephalous Orthodox, Greek Catholic |
| Exports: | Agricultural products—sugar, sugar beets, grain; raw materials—coal, iron, ore, manganese ore; consumer electronic equipment |
| Imports: | Oil, gas, medical equipment, food-processing machinery |
| Highest Point: | 6,800 ft. (2,073 m) |
| Lowest Point: | Sea level |
| Area: | 232,046 sq. mi. (600,999 sq km) |

# MOLDOVA

This territory under Soviet rule was known as Moldavia and, previously, Bessarabia. In the eighteenth and nineteenth centuries, the territory had been disputed between Turkey and Russia; in the twentieth century, it was ruled by Russia, except from 1918 to 1940 and 1941 to 1944 when the territory was part of Romania. The Romanian flag began to be flown again in 1989, and two years later Moldovan independence was proclaimed. In 1990, the blue-yellow-red vertical tricolor was officially adopted with the addition of a coat of arms in the center incorporating the eagle of Walachia and the ox head previously used in different forms by Moldavia, Bessarabia, Bukovina, and Chisinau (Kishinev), the capital of Moldova. Union with Romania in the future is possible.

# GEORGIA

In 1917 a national competition resulted in the creation of a flag for Georgia, designed by Jakob Nikola. The field of crimson or cherry red was said to stand for the bright past of the country and for joy. In the canton is a stripe of black, symbolic of the tragic era under Russian rule, and white, emblematic of peaceful developments and hope. The flag was officially adopted in 1918 when Georgia proclaimed its independence, but it disappeared three years later when the Red Army conquered Georgia. The flag was revived in the late 1980s, and in 1991 Georgia reasserted its independence. Of all the former Soviet republics, Georgia is alone in not participating in the Commonwealth of Independent States.

# ARMENIA

Long under Russian rule, Armenia proclaimed its independence in 1918 under a horizontal tricolor of red-blue-orange. Three years later the state disappeared when conquered by the Red Army. Although the Soviet regime later established a similar design, the Armenian tricolor was not flown legally until 1991. That year the country proclaimed its independence under the old flag.

| ARMENIA | |
| --- | --- |
| Official Name: | Republic of Armenia |
| Capital: | Yerevan |
| Languages: | Armenian |
| Religions: | Armenian Apostolic Church |
| Exports: | Copper, zinc, marble |
| Imports: | Petroleum products |
| Highest Point: | 13,419 ft. (4,090 m) |
| Lowest Point: | 1,280 ft. (390 m) |
| Area: | 11,506 sq. mi. (29,801 sq km) |

| MOLDOVA | |
| --- | --- |
| Official Name: | Republic of Moldova |
| Capital: | Kishinev |
| Languages: | Romanian, Russian |
| Religions: | Eastern Orthodox, Roman Catholic |
| Exports: | Wine, tobacco |
| Imports: | Unavailable at this time |
| Highest Point: | 1,407 ft. (429 m) |
| Lowest Point: | 3 ft. (0.9 m) above sea level |
| Area: | 13,012 sq. mi. (33,701 sq km) |

| GEORGIA | |
| --- | --- |
| Official Name: | Republic of Georgia |
| Capital: | Tbilisi |
| Languages: | Georgian |
| Religions: | Eastern Orthodox |
| Exports: | Wine, tea, tobacco, trucks, citrus fruit |
| Imports: | Wheat, meat, butter, consumer goods, agricultural machinery |
| Highest Point: | 16,627 ft. (5,068 m) |
| Lowest Point: | Sea level |
| Area: | 26,872 sq. mi. (69,598 sq km) |

# AZERBAIDZHAN

Introduced in 1917, the Azeri tricolor was officially recognized the following year when the independence of the nation was proclaimed. The poet Ali Bey Hussein Zade said that light blue represented the Turkic race of which Azeris are a part. The red symbolized the development of culture, and green recalled the Moslem faith of the people. The white star and crescent are similar to those found in the flags of neighboring Turkey, while the eight points of the star stand respectively for different branches of the Turkic race. The flag was revived in 1989 and became official in 1991, several months before the proclamation of Azeri independence.

| AZERBAIDZHAN | |
| --- | --- |
| Official Name: | Republic of Azerbaidzhan |
| Capital: | Baku |
| Languages: | Azeri |
| Religions: | Muslim |
| Exports: | Oil |
| Imports: | Unavailable at this time |
| Highest Point: | 14,652 ft. (4,466 m) |
| Lowest Point: | -92 ft. (-28 m) |
| Area: | 33,475 sq. mi. (86,700 sq km) |

# KAZAKHSTAN

Of all the Central Asian areas conquered by Russia in the eighteenth and nineteenth centuries, Kazakhstan was the one most heavily settled by Slavic peoples. When Kazakhstan became a separate Soviet republic in 1936, its flag differed from that of the Soviet Union only by having its name written in gold letters below the hammer and sickle. Finally, in 1953 a distinctive flag was adopted by Kazakhstan. To the Soviet flag was added near the bottom a light blue horizontal stripe. The stripe was said to stand for the sky and mountain peaks of the country, while the red was for the Communist revolution. The independence of Kazakhstan was proclaimed in 1991. A new flag undoubtedly will be adopted in the future.

| KAZAKHSTAN | |
| --- | --- |
| Official Name: | Republic of Kazakhstan |
| Capital: | Alma-Ata |
| Languages: | Turkic Chaghatay |
| Religions: | Muslim |
| Exports: | Oil, cotton |
| Imports: | Machinery, clothing, foodstuffs |
| Highest Point: | 22,949 ft. (6,995 m) |
| Lowest Point: | -433 ft. (-132 m) |
| Area: | 1,064,092 sq. mi. (2,756,000 sq km) |

# KYRGHYZSTAN

Known prior to Soviet rule as Kirghizia, this territory originally used a flag of red with its name, in Russian and Kyrghyz, in the upper left-hand corner in gold lettering. A similar flag was used when Kirghizia obtained the status of a Soviet Socialist Republic, one of fifteen constituting the USSR at the time of its dissolution in 1991. The present flag was adopted in 1952 by the addition of horizontal stripes of blue-white-blue through the center of the Soviet flag. The blue is said to stand for the mountains, the white for snow. Though a new national flag is expected, at the time of its proclamation of independence in 1991 Kyrghyzstan had not developed a new design.

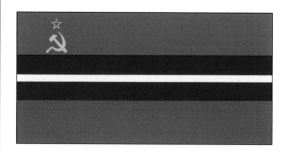

| KYRGHYZSTAN | |
| --- | --- |
| Official Name: | Republic of Kyrghyzstan |
| Capital: | Bishkek |
| Languages: | Turkic Chaghatay |
| Religions: | Muslim |
| Exports: | Minerals |
| Imports: | Machinery, clothing, foodstuffs |
| Highest Point: | 23,406 ft. (7,134 m) |
| Lowest Point: | 1,800 ft. (549 m) |
| Area: | 76,641 sq. mi. (198,500 sq km) |

# TADZHIKISTAN

The first Tadzhik flag, adopted in 1929, had its coat of arms in the upper hoist corner of a red banner. In 1935, 1937, and 1940 a simpler flag—bearing the name of the state in gold lettering on a red background—was made official in slightly different versions. Finally, in 1953 the current flag was adopted. To the flag of the USSR were added horizontal stripes of white and green. White was for cotton, the most important agricultural product, while green recalled the other farm produce of this Central Asian nation. The flag was not altered in 1991 at the time independence was proclaimed, but a new design will probably be selected.

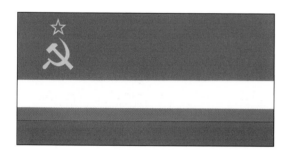

| TADZHIKISTAN | |
|---|---|
| Official Name: | Republic of Tadzhikistan |
| Capital: | Dushanbe |
| Languages: | Turkic Chaghatay |
| Religions: | Muslim |
| Exports: | Cotton, gold, uranium |
| Imports: | Machinery, clothing, foodstuffs |
| Highest Point: | 24,590 ft. (7,495 m) |
| Lowest Point: | 985 ft. (300 m) |
| Area: | 55,019 sq. mi. (142,499 sq km) |

# UZBEKISTAN

The Soviet Uzbek flag adopted in 1952 had stripes of red at the top and bottom, with a white-bordered light blue stripe running through the center. In the upper corner were the hammer, sickle, and star of communism. When independence was proclaimed in 1991 a new flag was developed on the basis of the old one. The five horizontal stripes were retained but were given different colors, while a crescent and twelve stars substituted for the Soviet symbols. The light blue is a symbol of water and the sky, while green is an emblem of nature and spring. (Blue and green also recall the Turkic race and Moslem religion of the people.) White is for peace, and red is for the life force. The stars are for the twelve months of the year, and the new moon is for the growth of a new republic. The crescent and stars are omitted on the reverse side of the flag.

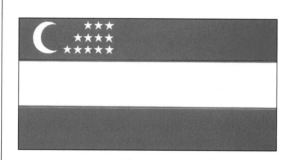

| UZBEKISTAN | |
|---|---|
| Official Name: | Republic of Uzbekistan |
| Capital: | Tashkent |
| Languages: | Turkic Chaghatay |
| Religions: | Muslim |
| Exports: | Cotton, gold, uranium |
| Imports: | Machinery, clothing, foodstuffs |
| Highest Point: | 15,233 ft. (4,643 m) |
| Lowest Point: | -39 ft. (-12 m) |
| Area: | 158,069 sq. mi. (409,399 sq km) |

# TURKMENISTAN

The original Turkmen flag was a version of the Soviet Red Banner with the hammer, sickle, and star in the upper hoist corner. In 1937 a new design was adopted. The red flag bore the initials of the state (T.C.C.P.) in gold Cyrillic lettering in the upper hoist corner. Finally, in 1956 a distinctive flag was created, again based on that of the USSR. Running through the center were two light blue horizontal stripes. These are said to stand for the irrigation systems of the republic which bring life to agriculture and the native population. The flag was not changed when the independence of Turkmenistan was proclaimed in 1991.

| TURKMENISTAN | |
|---|---|
| Official Name: | Republic of Turkmenistan |
| Capital: | Ashkhabad |
| Languages: | Turkic Chaghatay |
| Religions: | Muslim |
| Exports: | Cotton, gold, uranium, natural gas |
| Imports: | Machinery, clothing, foodstuffs |
| Highest Point: | 10,299 ft. (3,139 m) |
| Lowest Point: | -266 ft. (-81 m) |
| Area: | 188,417 sq. mi. (488,000 sq km) |

## LITHUANIA

In the fourteenth century, the grand duchy of Lithuania had a red shield with a white mounted knight in the center as its coat of arms. A flag of the same design was also flown, and that design was revived as the state flag of Lithuania under the independent republic of 1918–1940. The national flag in that era, however, was a simple horizontal tricolor of yellow, green, and red. The colors were said to stand for the ripening wheat, the forests, and the flowers of the land. The flag was created in 1918 and officially adopted in 1922, but was suppressed under Soviet rule from 1940 until 1988. In 1990 the independence of Lithuania was proclaimed under this banner, but it was more than a year and a half before the country obtained international recognition and Soviet acquiescence.

| LITHUANIA | |
|---|---|
| Official Name: | Republic of Lithuania |
| Capital: | Vilnius |
| Languages: | Lithuanian |
| Religions: | Roman Catholic, Lutheran |
| Exports: | Building materials |
| Imports: | Fuels |
| Highest Point: | 965 ft. (294 m) |
| Lowest Point: | Sea level |
| Area: | 25,174 sq. mi. (65,200 sq km) |

## LATVIA

Latvia's distinctive maroon flag with a narrow white stripe is claimed to be one of the oldest in the world. According to tradition, the flag is found in a rhymed chronicle dating from 1279, although Latvians believe the flag is much older. The flag was revived in 1870, but could not be flown because the territory was then part of the Russian Empire. In 1918, Latvia proclaimed its independence, and the flag was officially reestablished in 1922. In 1940, Soviet power was imposed and the flag disappeared, although Latvians in exile continued to display it. In 1988 it was again legalized, entirely replacing the Soviet Latvian flag in 1990. When independence was revived in 1991, the Latvian flag was hoisted at the United Nations.

| LATVIA | |
|---|---|
| Official Name: | Republic of Latvia |
| Capital: | Riga |
| Languages: | Latvian, Russian |
| Religions: | Lutheran, Eastern Orthodox, Roman Catholic |
| Exports: | Steel, foodstuffs, appliances |
| Imports: | Fuel |
| Highest Point: | 655 ft. (200 m) |
| Lowest Point: | Sea level |
| Area: | 24,595 sq. mi. (63,701 sq km) |

## ESTONIA

In 1881, students of Estonia, then part of the Russian Empire, adopted the blue-black-white tricolor. A native folk song says that the stripes stand respectively for the sky, the soil, and the aspiration to freedom. National song festivals kept the flag alive until 1918, when the independence of Estonia was proclaimed. The flag was officially adopted in 1920, but disappeared two decades later when the Soviet Union annexed Estonia. In 1988, the flag was revived when more liberal policies in the Soviet Union allowed for expressions of nationalism. Two years later, the blue-black-white was officially readopted to replace the Soviet Estonian flag. In 1991, Estonia reestablished its independence, and this was internationally recognized.

| ESTONIA | |
|---|---|
| Official Name: | Republic of Estonia |
| Capital: | Tallin |
| Languages: | Estonian, Russian |
| Religions: | Lutheran, Eastern Orthodox |
| Exports: | Light industrial products, foodstuffs, machinery, chemical products, paper, furniture |
| Imports: | Fuel, raw materials |
| Highest Point: | 1,000 ft. (305 m) |
| Lowest Point: | Sea level |
| Area: | 17,413 sq. mi. (45,100 sq km) |

# NORTH KOREA

North Korea became independent of foreign occupation and adopted its new flag, whose design is governed by its constitution, in 1948. North Korea's flag has kept the red, white, and blue of the old flag of Korea, but with more emphasis on the red than the white. The red represents the revolution; the white, purity and simplicity; and the blue, peace and progress. The red star symbolizes the leadership of the Communist party. Additionally, the red star in the white disk is also believed to be the communist version of the *t'aeguk*, the yin-yang emblem found on the flag of South Korea.

| NORTH KOREA | |
|---|---|
| Official Name: | Democratic People's Republic of Korea |
| Capital: | Pyongyang |
| Languages: | Korean |
| Religions: | Buddhist, Confucian |
| Exports: | Minerals, machinery, textile fibers |
| Imports: | Petroleum, machinery, food, coal |
| Highest Point: | 9,003 ft. (2,744 m) |
| Lowest Point: | Sea level |
| Area: | 46,540 sq. mi. (120,492 sq km) |

# SOUTH KOREA

South Korea became independent in 1948. It has retained but altered the flag of the former Kingdom of Korea, which was originally adopted near the end of the nineteenth century by the emperor of Korea. The colors and shape of the yin-yang were established by law in 1948, and the four *kwae* were slightly revised in 1950. The yin-yang symbol, created by the Chinese philosopher Chu-Hsi, is a commonly known symbol for the balance of opposites and is widely used in Japan and China; a version of the yin-yang also appears on the flag of Mongolia (see **Mongolia**). The trigrams are the basic ones used in the *I Ching* (often called the *Book of Changes*), a system, also popular in the East, used to predict the future or to find solutions to dilemmas. The four trigrams that appear on the flag of South Korea represent heaven (upper hoist); water (upper fly); fire (lower hoist); and earth (lower fly). In 1984, the flag's layout was slightly revised to appear as it does today.

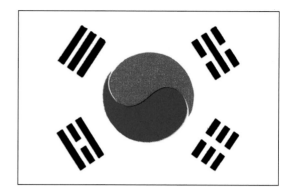

| SOUTH KOREA | |
|---|---|
| Official Name: | Republic of Korea |
| Capital: | Seoul |
| Languages: | Korean |
| Religions: | Buddhist, Christian, shamanistic, Confucian |
| Exports: | Textiles, transportation equipment, footwear |
| Imports: | Petroleum, machinery, transportation equipment, chemicals |
| Highest Point: | 6,398 ft. (1,950 m) |
| Lowest Point: | Sea level |
| Area: | 38,025 sq. mi. (98,447 sq km) |

© Steve Vidler/Leo de Wys, Inc.

*The statue of a warrior decorates a Korean temple in Kyongju.*

# JAPAN

Japan, whose name means "the source of the sun" and is often called "the Land of the Rising Sun," has been an independent nation since ancient times. The flag of Japan carries a *mon* (see page 14), called *Hinomaru*, which translated means "the Disc of the Sun." The emperors believe themselves to be descendants of the sun goddess, Amaterasu Omikami, and the sun disk has been an imperial badge since the 1300s.

Only since 1854 has the sun disk been Japan's national symbol. The year before, Japan finally opened its doors to the West and permitted United States Commodore Matthew Perry to visit. After this the Shogun (the military commander) of the House of Tokugawa made the image available for use on merchant ships. Before 1854, a samurai warrior carried his flag, which bore his family heraldic emblem, on his back. In 1870, the *Hinomaru* became the legal national flag of Japan. In 1889, Japan adopted use of the Rising Sun flag, which was used by the Japanese navy and military; however, this flag was outlawed at the end of World War II. The Rising Sun flag was later revived in 1954 for the Maritime Defense Force and is used today for the Ground Self-Defense Force.

The white background of the *Hinomaru* is said to represent purity and integrity, while the red stands for brightness, sincerity, and warmth. The flag, therefore, symbolizes the national ideal of *Akaki kiyoki tadashiki naoki makoto no kokoro* (Bright, pure, just and gentle of heart). Japan also has three different sets of proportions for its flag; each version places the disk at varying distances to the hoist. In Japan, flags are often used on holidays and feast days as well as to greet the emperor.

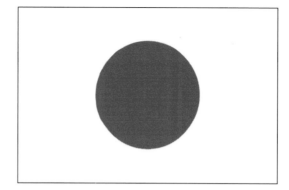

| **JAPAN** | |
|---|---|
| Official Name: | Japan |
| Capital: | Tokyo |
| Languages: | Japanese |
| Religions: | Shinto, Buddhist, others |
| Exports: | Machinery, motor vehicles, textiles |
| Imports: | Petroleum, raw materials, food, machinery |
| Highest Point: | 12,388 ft. (3,776 m) |
| Lowest Point: | -13 ft. (-4 m) |
| Area: | 145,834 sq. mi. (377,564 sq km) |

*ABOVE: The military flag of Japan adds rays to the sun disk of the national flag.*

*BELOW: Mount Fuji is the most popular pilgrimage site for Japanese.*

*ABOVE, LEFT: Downtown Tokyo is a scene of constant activity day and night.*

*LEFT: The distinctive and highly stylized art of Japan, like this Utamaro painting, now has an international audience.*

*ABOVE, RIGHT: Sightseeing Japanese sailors emerge from St. Paul's Cathedral in London.*

*RIGHT: The Japanese flag flies before a carved tower at the Sapporo Snow Festival.*

## *TAIWAN*

Taiwan, also referred to as Nationalist China, uses a flag in which the red symbolizes the land of China itself, or the Han Chinese (versus other Chinese ethnic groups). The white sun represents the spirit of progress while the twelve points represent the twelve hours of the day. The emblem of the white sun on the blue field is the flag of the Kuo Min Tang Nationalist party, and was designed by Sun Yat-sen, who founded the party in 1891. In 1928 Chiang Kai-shek reunified China and reorganized its government. At that time the new national flag was adopted; it consisted of a red field with a party flag of the Kuo Min Tang (a white sun on a blue field) as the canton. Chiang Kai-shek's government was at war with both the Communists and the Japanese from the 1930s until 1949, at which time it was driven off the mainland to the island of Taiwan, where, despite the lack of recognition by the world's major countries, it thrives to this day. The 1928 flags are still in use there as well.

| TAIWAN | |
|---|---|
| Official Name: | Republic of China |
| Capital: | Taipei |
| Languages: | Chinese dialects |
| Religions: | Buddhist, Confucian, Taoist, Christian |
| Exports: | Textiles, electrical machinery, plastics, plywood |
| Imports: | Petroleum, machinery, chemicals, food |
| Highest Point: | 13,113 ft. (3,997 m) |
| Lowest Point: | Sea level |
| Area: | 13,900 sq. mi. (35,987 sq km) |

## *PHILIPPINES*

The Philippines became independent from foreign occupation in 1946, but had sought freedom since 1898, the year the flag was designed by General Emilio Aguinaldo. The flag was adopted by a faction of exiled Filipinos who were in Hong Kong planning a revolt against Spanish rule.

Under American administration the flag was illegal from 1907 until 1919, and under the Japanese it was forbidden between 1941 and 1942. Under the commonwealth established by the Americans, the flag had legal recognition and was readopted in 1943 under the Japanese-sponsored "Second Republic." The blue stands for noble ideals, the red for courage and bravery, and the white for peace and purity. The stars symbolize the three main regions of the country (Luzon, Visayan, Mindanao), while the eight rays of the sun represent the first eight provinces to rebel against Spanish tyranny. The triangle represents equality. In times of war, the flag is flown with the red color atop the blue.

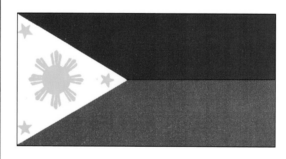

| PHILIPPINES | |
|---|---|
| Official Name: | Republic of the Philippines |
| Capital: | Manila |
| Languages: | Filipino, Spanish, English, Malaysian-Polynesian |
| Religions: | Roman Catholic, Protestant, Muslim, Buddhist |
| Exports: | Coconut products, sugar, wood, textiles |
| Imports: | Petroleum, industrial equipment, wheat |
| Highest Point: | 9,692 ft. (2,954 m) |
| Lowest Point: | Sea level |
| Area: | 115,831 sq. mi. (299,886 sq km) |

## *BRUNEI*

Brunei became independent from Britain in 1984, but its national flag dates back to 1906. Before 1906, Brunei had no national flag, but used several different flags, one for each sultan and state official. When the national flag was designed, it was said that the flag's yellow field represented the royal sultan, while the black and white diagonals symbolized the two senior state officials.

The national emblem, added in 1959, depicts a winged mast with an umbrella and flag on top, centered between the horns of a crescent moon with the state motto, "Always render service with God's guidance," written in Jawi. The inscription on the scroll, also in Jawi script, says "Brunei, city of peace." The dual hands, which represent the benevolence of the government, were added to the emblem at the time it was added to the flag.

| BRUNEI | |
|---|---|
| Official Name: | State of Brunei Darussalam |
| Capital: | Bandar Seri Begawan |
| Languages: | Malay, English, Chinese |
| Religions: | Muslim, Christian, Buddhist, others |
| Exports: | Petroleum, natural gas |
| Imports: | Machinery, transportation equipment, manufactured goods, food |
| Highest Point: | 6,070 ft. (1,850 m) |
| Lowest Point: | Sea level |
| Area: | 2,226 sq. mi. (5,763 sq km) |

# MALAYSIA

The Federation of Malaysia was formed in September 1963 and, at that time, included the eleven states of Malaya, Singapore, Sabah (formerly North Borneo), and Sarawak (northwest Borneo). The flag of Malaysia is a unique combination of the crescent and star, traditional Islamic symbols, and the Stars and Stripes of the United States. From 1957 until 1963, the region used a flag with only eleven stripes and an eleven-pointed star; however, after Malaysia was formed, the other three stripes and star points were added. Then, the fourteen stripes and the fourteen-pointed star symbolized the member states, but after Singapore left the federation to become an independent nation in 1965, the fourteenth stripe and point were redefined to represent the federal territories. The blue canton represents the nation's affiliation to the Commonwealth, while the yellow is the color of the royal sultans. The red and white colors have been used for hundreds of years in the area and are found in the flags of neighboring Indonesia, Singapore, Philippines, and Thailand.

| | MALAYSIA |
|---|---|
| Official Name: | Federation of Malaysia |
| Capital: | Kuala Lumpur |
| Languages: | Malay, Chinese dialects, Tamil, English |
| Religions: | Muslim, Buddhist, Hindu, Confucian, Christian |
| Exports: | Petroleum, natural rubber, wood, palm oil |
| Imports: | Machinery, food, transportation equipment, manufactured goods |
| Highest Point: | 13,455 ft. (4,101 m) |
| Lowest Point: | Sea level |
| Area: | 128,430 sq. mi. (332,505 sq km) |

# SINGAPORE

Singapore became independent within the Federation of Malaysia in 1963 (see **Malaysia**) and gained separate independence in 1965. The flag, adopted in 1959, when Singapore was a British possession, was preserved upon independence and is identical to the flag of Indonesia except for the white crescent and stars. The colors, which are also the Malay colors, represent the brotherhood of man (red), and purity and virtue (white). The crescent on this flag symbolizes a young country. The five stars represent the ideals of democracy, peace, progress, justice, and equality.

| | SINGAPORE |
|---|---|
| Official Name: | Republic of Singapore |
| Capital: | Singapore |
| Languages: | English, Chinese, Malay, Tamil |
| Religions: | Buddhist, Taoist, Muslim, Hindu, Christian |
| Exports: | Petroleum products, electrical machinery, rubber |
| Imports: | Machinery, petroleum, manufactured goods, rice |
| Highest Point: | 545 ft. (166 m) |
| Lowest Point: | Sea level |
| Area: | 224 sq. mi. (580 sq km) |

# INDONESIA

Indonesia proclaimed its independence after Japan's surrender in 1945, but four years elapsed before it actually attained it. The flag's colors have a dual history—both the red and the white are attributed to Prince Jayakatong during the thirteenth century. A red-and-white flag also was used by Indonesian freedom fighters who revolted against Dutch control from 1928 until 1941, when Japan began its four-year occupation of the country.

| | INDONESIA |
|---|---|
| Official Name: | Republic of Indonesia |
| Capital: | Jakarta |
| Languages: | Bahasa Indonesian, Malayo-Polynesian, English, Dutch |
| Religions: | Muslim, Christian, Hindu |
| Exports: | Petroleum, natural gas, wood, rubber |
| Imports: | Food, machinery, chemicals, transportation equipment |
| Highest Point: | 16,503 ft. (5,030 m) |
| Lowest Point: | Sea level |
| Area: | 741,101 sq. mi. (1,918,710 sq km) |

*TOP, CENTER: Chinese traditions—including the New Year's dragon—are popular in Singapore.*

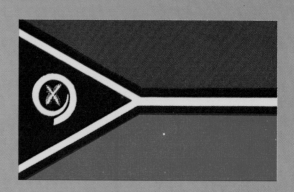

# CHAPTER FOUR

# *Australia*

There is a constellation that is visible in the skies of the Southern Hemisphere, and for hundreds of years it has served as a navigational aid to fishermen, sailors, and others at sea. The Southern Cross, as that constellation is called, also has been a consistent symbol in Australian flags since the early 1800s.

In Australia, the national colonial flag of 1823 was the first flag to carry the four stars of the Southern Cross. This flag placed the four stars on the red cross of the British White Ensign. The New South Wales Ensign appeared in 1831. This flag resembled the former, except that the central cross was blue and bore five stars instead of four. Later in the nineteenth century it came to represent the movement towards federation of all the Australian territories—New South Wales, Queensland, Victoria, South Australia, Western Australia, and Tasmania.

In 1854, gold miners unsuccessfully fought for electoral reforms and for a more equitable licensing system for mining. They formed the Ballarat Reform League, which used a blue flag with a white cross and five white eight-pointed stars. This flag was hoisted over the Eureka Stockade, where the rebel miners resisted the state militia. While the revolt was unsuccessful, it did cause the creation of a reform league that mediated disputes between the government and the miners. The revolt at the

Eureka Stockade became famous, and the flag came to symbolize radical ideas, particularly those associated with making Australia a republic. This flag design is still popular in Australia today.

On January 1, 1901, Australia became a federal dominion and a competition was staged to find an appropriate national flag. A total of 32,823 designs were submitted, and the winning design was actually entered by five different people. The winning flag consisted of three distinct parts: the Union Flag (illustrating Australia's tie with Britain), the Southern Cross (for Australia) on a blue background, and the Commonwealth Star (for the six member states). One of the stars had, and still has, only five points, indicating that it is not as bright as the other stars in the actual constellation. In 1908, the Commonwealth Star's six points were altered to seven in order to represent all Australian territories as well as the six states, and the symbol now represents the entire federation.

In 1903, the flag (with a red background) was officially adopted for use on Australian vessels, and in 1954, the blue version finally became the official national flag of Australia.

Today, each of Australia's six states has its own flag based on the blue British Ensign. Each flag flies in its canton a small Union Flag and has a royal blue field. The emblem on each flag is modeled after the individual state's coat of arms. Three of Australia's dependencies (Northern Territory [now self-governing], Christmas Island, and Norfolk Island) also have their own flags. The Cocos Islands and Australian Antarctic Territory do not have flags of their own.

| AUSTRALIA | |
|---|---|
| Official Name: | Commonwealth of Australia |
| Capital: | Canberra |
| Languages: | English |
| Religions: | Anglican, Roman Catholic, Protestant |
| Exports: | Coal, wood, wheat |
| Imports: | Capital equipment, consumer goods, transportation equipment |
| Highest Point: | 7,310 ft. (2,228 m) |
| Lowest Point: | -52 ft. (-16 m) |
| Area: | 2,967,909 sq. mi. (7,683,916 sq km) |

*RIGHT: The first British settlement in Australia occurred in 1788 at Botany Bay.*

*OPPOSITE: The Parliament Building in Canberra, Australian Capital Territory.*

*RIGHT: The Opera House in Sydney has become a landmark for Australia's largest city.*

*BELOW: Ayer's Rock in central Australia is famous for changing colors under different light conditions.*

© Steve Vidler/Leo de Wys, Inc.

# Australian States and Dependencies

## New South Wales

The flag emblem of New South Wales, which dates back to 1876, consists of St. George's cross with the gold lion of England in its center. An eight-pointed star is on each arm of the cross.

## Queensland

Queensland's emblem displays a crown in the center of a blue Maltese cross on a white field. This emblem was introduced in 1876.

## South Australia

South Australia's flag emblem depicts a regional bird with outstretched wings, the white-backed piping shrike. The emblem was introduced in 1904.

## Tasmania

Tasmania, formerly called Van Diemen's Land, was named for Abel Tasman, who discovered the region in 1642 while exploring on behalf of the Dutch East India Company. This flag uses a lion emblem, which was introduced in 1876.

## Northern Territory

This region uses a flag that was created in 1978 and was designed by two graphic artists. The hoist is black with stars that resemble those of Victoria, while the fly bears a stylized Sturt's desert rose on an ochre field.

## Victoria

Victoria's original flag emblem, introduced in 1870, carried only the Southern Cross without the Royal Crown. In 1877, the crown was added to the fly.

## Western Australia

Western Australia's black swan emblem was first used by the Swan River Colony. It was introduced as the state's emblem in 1875; in 1953, the swan was turned around to face the hoist.

## Norfolk Island

Norfolk Island is a dependency that lies east of Australia in the Pacific Ocean. This island adopted its Norfolk Island pine emblem in 1980; however, the pine was first used on a seal in 1856.

## Christmas Island

Christmas Island is a dependency that lies south of Java in the Indian Ocean. This island's flag is unofficial and for internal use only. The stars depicted on the flag are the same as the stars on the flag of Australia. A map of the island is in the center of the flag. A frigate bird is seen on the upper fly.

## Aboriginal Flag

Australia has a flag that is used as an ethnic flag by native-born Aborigines and to symbolize their desire for land reform that grants them rights to their land. This flag was developed in 1972 as a part of the Land Rights Campaign. The colors represent the following: black, the people; red, the land and the blood shed by the Aborigines in defense of it; and the yellow disk symbolizes the sun.

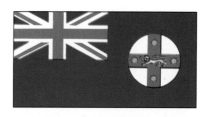

**NEW SOUTH WALES STATE FLAG**

**QUEENSLAND STATE FLAG**

**SOUTH AUSTRALIA STATE FLAG**

**TASMANIA STATE FLAG**

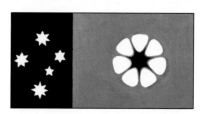

**NORTHERN TERRITORY FLAG**

**VICTORIA STATE FLAG**

**WESTERN AUSTRALIA FLAG**

Courtesy of Australian Consulate General

© James K. Hackett/Leo de Wys, Inc.

© Gary Bell/The Wildlife Collection

**ABOVE:** *The Great Barrier Reef off the eastern coast of Australia is the world's largest coral reef.*

**TOP, RIGHT:** *Many species of reef fish inhabit the Great Barrier Reef.*

© Gerry Ellis/The Wildlife Collection

**RIGHT:** *Erskine Falls, Otway Ranges, Victoria.*

**FAR RIGHT:** *The Koala bear feeds only on the leaves of the eucalyptus tree.*

© Norman Isaacs/Envision

# NEW ZEALAND

New Zealand's first flag was adopted at Waitangi in 1834, before it became a British colony. This flag consisted of a red St. George's cross on a white background, with a canton of blue. A black-bordered red cross separated four white eight-pointed stars in the canton. This flag was used until 1840, when New Zealand became a British colony and British ensigns were flown. From 1867 until 1869, the letters 'NZ' in red and white borders made up the badge.

The present flag was adopted as the New Zealand government ensign in 1869 and became the national flag in 1902. New Zealand became independent in 1907. Originally, the Red Ensign had red stars on a white disk; however, in 1903, the ensign was altered to depict white stars against a red field. Red and white are common colors in Maori flags; perhaps for this reason the British Red Ensign is frequently used inland by the Maoris.

New Zealand has two self-governing dependencies, the Cook Islands and Niue.

ABOVE: A view of the city of Queenstown, New Zealand.

RIGHT: Milford Sound on the South Island of New Zealand.

| NEW ZEALAND | |
|---|---|
| Official Name: | New Zealand |
| Capital: | Wellington |
| Languages: | English, Maori |
| Religions: | Anglican, Presbyterian, Roman Catholic, others |
| Exports: | Wool, meat and dairy products, wood products |
| Imports: | Machinery, manufactured goods, petroleum, motor vehicles |
| Highest Point: | 12,349 ft. (3,764 m) |
| Lowest Point: | Sea level |
| Area: | 103,515 sq. mi. (268,000 sq km) |

*RIGHT: A Maori carving. The Maori people of New Zealand came from Polynesia hundreds of years ago.*

*LEFT: Glaciers, water-falls, mountain lakes, and forests are part of New Zealand's beautiful scenery. Bowen Falls on South Island's Milford Sound is shown here.*

*BELOW: Sheep raising is an important part of the New Zealand economy.*

## COOK ISLANDS

The Cook Islands are comprised of fifteen Pacific Ocean islands that, while still dependent upon New Zealand for defense and foreign affairs, became self-governing in 1965. These islands have flown many different flags, two of which used a ring of fifteen stars, one for each island. The previous flag, adopted in 1974, when the islands achieved internal government, carried a ring of yellow stars on an otherwise plain green field. The present flag was adopted in 1979, when the Cook Island party lost power to the Democratic party, whose colors are white and blue.

## NIUE

The island of Niue was once a part of the Cook Islands, but in 1974 became a self-governing dependency of New Zealand and adopted its flag the following year. The Union Flag is a reminder of the time when Niue was a British protectorate. The four stars symbolize the Southern Cross and, therefore, the island's connection to New Zealand. The large star centered in the blue disk represents the island itself, "alone within the deep blue sea."

# WESTERN SAMOA

Several flags incorporating the colors red and white, and sometimes blue, were used by Samoa prior to 1873. That year a red flag with a white cross extending to the edges and a white star in the upper hoist corner was adopted. In 1886, this was replaced by a cross of black with white and black borders on a field of white. The canton remained red with a white star. During 1889, Samoa was a tripartite protectorate, jointly ruled by the United States, Britain, and Germany. Samoa was occupied by Germany from 1900 until 1914, when it became a New Zealand mandate, a status that lasted until 1962. In 1948, New Zealand created a flag for this territory, one which, like its own flag, used the stars of the Southern Cross. The fifth, smaller star was added in 1949. The nation gained final independence, after many years as a territory protected by the United Nations, in 1962.

| WESTERN SAMOA | |
|---|---|
| Official Name: | Independent State of Western Samoa |
| Capital: | Apia |
| Languages: | Samoan, English |
| Religions: | Christian |
| Exports: | Copra, cocoa, wood, bananas |
| Imports: | Food, manufactured goods, petroleum, machinery |
| Highest Point: | 6,096 ft. (1,858 m) |
| Lowest Point: | Sea level |
| Area: | 1,097 sq. mi. (2,840 sq km) |

# PAPUA NEW GUINEA

Papua New Guinea was originally divided into German and Australian territories. In 1921, the German territory was transferred to Australia, but not before Germany introduced the use of the bird of paradise as the colony's emblem. This emblem resurfaced on a flag used in 1962. In 1970, the government proposed a flag consisting of vertical stripes of blue-yellow-green bearing the stars of the Southern Cross on the blue and a silhouette bird of paradise on the green.

In the course of displaying this flag throughout the country, the government discovered a design created by Susan Karike. Her design was considered better than the blue-yellow-green one and eventually was adopted officially as the national flag. This flag has the unusual proportions of 3:4 and each of its five-pointed white stars are of different sizes, much like the stars on the flag of Western Samoa (see **Western Samoa**). The colors are popular and regularly used in native art.

| PAPUA NEW GUINEA | |
|---|---|
| Official Name: | Independent State of Papua New Guinea |
| Capital: | Port Moresby |
| Languages: | English, Papuan, Negrito |
| Religions: | Roman Catholic, Lutheran, indigenous |
| Exports: | Copper, coffee beans, coconut products |
| Imports: | Machinery, manufactured goods, petroleum, food |
| Highest Point: | 14,793 ft. (4,439 m) |
| Lowest Point: | Sea level |
| Area: | 178,703 sq. mi. (462,662 sq km) |

# VANUATU

Vanuatu was known as New Hebrides until 1980, when it became independent from joint rule by France and Britain (which had governed the islands since 1906) and took on its present name. From 1906 to 1980, the Anglo-French condominium flew the Tricolor side by side with the Union Flag. Before independence in 1980, the dominant Vanuaaku party chose a flag for the new state, which they intended to name after themselves. This flag had red and black triangles with a stripe of green at the hoist with orange native tools. However, at the actual time of independence, the inhabitants opted for the name Vanuatu and adopted a different version of the flag. This particular version retained the colors and the triangles, but added the boar's tusk (worn by many islanders as a pendant to symbolize prosperity) and the crossed *namele* fern leaves, which symbolize peace.

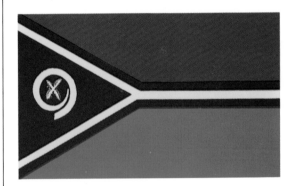

| VANUATU | |
|---|---|
| Official Name: | Republic of Vanuatu |
| Capital: | Vila |
| Languages: | Bislama, English |
| Religions: | Christian |
| Exports: | Copra, frozen fish, meat |
| Imports: | Food, manufactured goods, fuels |
| Highest Point: | 6,165 ft. (1,879 m) |
| Lowest Point: | Sea level |
| Area: | 5,714 sq. mi. (14,794 sq km) |

# THE SOLOMON ISLANDS

The Solomon Islands were a British protectorate from 1893 to 1978, when they became self-governing. As a British protectorate, the islands used the Union Jack and also special British ensigns. The earliest ensign badge had the royal crown surrounded by the words "British Solomon Islands." In 1947 a coat of arms was developed that bore a turtle, but was objected to because it was representative of only a part of the local inhabitants. In 1956, a complicated shield with weapons, turtles, an eagle, and a lion was adopted.

The present flag was chosen after a lengthy debate over its design and a semi-official competition. The flag's five stars do not symbolize the stars of the Southern Cross, but the five major groups of islands within the country. The color green represents the country's land and vegetation. The color yellow symbolizes its sunshine.

| SOLOMON ISLANDS | |
|---|---|
| Official Name: | Solomon Islands |
| Capital: | Honiara |
| Languages: | English, Malaysian-Polynesian |
| Religions: | Anglican, Roman Catholic, Methodist, Christian |
| Exports: | Copra, wood, fish, palm oil |
| Imports: | Machinery, transportation equipment, food, fuels |
| Highest Point: | 8,028 ft. (2,447 m) |
| Lowest Point: | Sea level |
| Area: | 11,506 sq. mi. (29,789 sq km) |

# NAURU

Before independence in 1968, Nauru was a tripartite trusteeship of Britain, Australia, and New Zealand and flew the flags of these countries alongside another. Prior to independence, a local design competition was held and the present design, which was not based on any earlier concepts or symbols, was chosen. The flag's blue color represents the sky and the Pacific Ocean, while the yellow stripe represents the equator. The twelve-pointed star symbolizes Nauru, which has twelve original tribes. The star's placement on the field is meant to illustrate the country's geographical position, which is one degree south of the equator.

| NAURU | |
|---|---|
| Official Name: | Republic of Nauru |
| Capital: | Yaren District |
| Languages: | Nauruan, English |
| Religions: | Protestant, Roman Catholic |
| Exports: | Phosphates |
| Imports: | Food, fuels, water |
| Highest Point: | 213 ft. (65 m) |
| Lowest Point: | Sea level |
| Area: | 8 sq. mi. (21 sq km) |

# TONGA

Tonga, often called "the Friendly Islands," became a unified kingdom in 1845. Its national flag was adopted in 1862; in keeping with the wishes of King George Tupou I, who introduced it, the flag is protected by the constitution of Tonga and has remained unchanged throughout the years. The design replaced a previous flag that had a white field with four Greek crosses (the Greek cross has four equal arms), two in red and two in blue. The red and white col-

ors are the colors of Polynesia, while the cross symbolizes the monarch's and the nation's adherence to Christianity.

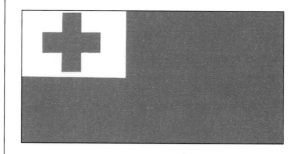

| TONGA | |
|---|---|
| Official Name: | Kingdom of Tonga |
| Capital: | Nuku Alofa |
| Languages: | Tongan, English |
| Religions: | Christian |
| Exports: | Copra, bananas, coconut products |
| Imports: | Food, machinery, petroleum |
| Highest Point: | 3,380 ft. (1,030 m) |
| Lowest Point: | Sea level |
| Area: | 270 sq. mi. (699 sq km) |

# FIJI

The Fiji Islands were ceded to Britain in 1874; prior to that time, the country was a united kingdom under Chief Cakobau. Under Cakobau, Fiji flew a flag that was vertically blue and white with a crowned shield in the center. After 1874, the nation flew British ensigns, and added its arms as an emblem in 1908.

A flag design competition was held at the time of independence in 1970, at which point the present flag was chosen. This flag carries the Union Flag on its canton to symbolize Fiji's connection to the Commonwealth. On the fly is the shield of Fiji, which displays St. George's cross and several emblems: three sugar canes, a coconut palm, a bunch of bananas, and a dove with an olive branch in its beak. Above these symbols is a lion holding a coconut.

In 1987, Fiji left the Commonwealth. Since a new constitution is now being worked out, it is probable that a new flag will be adopted.

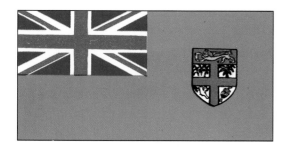

| FIJI | |
|---|---|
| Official Name: | Fiji |
| Capital: | Suva |
| Languages: | English, Fijian, Hindustani |
| Religions: | Christian, Hindu, Muslim |
| Exports: | Sugar, copra |
| Imports: | Machinery, food, fuels |
| Highest Point: | 4,341 ft. (1,302 m) |
| Lowest Point: | Sea level |
| Area: | 7,055 sq. mi. (18,265 sq km) |

# TUVALU

Tuvalu (which means "The Nine Islands") was once called the Ellice Islands. From 1892 to 1975, Tuvalu and the Gilbert Islands (now called Kiribati), were administered by Britain (Tuvalu gained separate colony status in 1975). During this eighty-three-year period, Tuvalu flew the British Union Flag. From 1976, when Tuvalu obtained its own coat of arms, until independence in 1978, the coat of arms was used as a flag badge. Prior to independence, Tuvalu held a design competition for a national flag; the winning entry, in use today, carries the British Union flag, symbolizing membership in the British Commonwealth, and nine stars, representing the nine islands that make up the country. The pattern of the stars closely resembles the actual geographic pattern of the islands.

| TUVALU | |
|---|---|
| Official Name: | Tuvalu |
| Capital: | Funafuti |
| Languages: | Tuvaluan, English |
| Religions: | Christian |
| Exports: | Copra |
| Imports: | Food, fuels |
| Highest Point: | 15 ft. (5 m) |
| Lowest Point: | Sea level |
| Area: | 10 sq. mi. (26 sq km) |

# KIRIBATI

Kiribati (pronounced KIR-i-bass) was once a part of the Gilbert and Ellice Islands colony that was ruled and administered by Britain. Kiribati was granted self-rule in 1971 and won total independence in 1979. The flag, chosen in a design competition, is unusual in that it is a version of the country's arms in flag form (this type of flag is called an armorial flag). The frigate bird, which also appears on the arms is slightly larger on the flag and symbolizes freedom and power.

| KIRIBATI | |
|---|---|
| Official Name: | Republic of Kiribati |
| Capital: | Bairiki |
| Languages: | English, Gilbertese |
| Religions: | Roman Catholic, Protestant |
| Exports: | Copra, fish |
| Imports: | Food, fuels, transportation equipment |
| Highest Point: | 265 ft. (81 m) |
| Lowest Point: | Sea level |
| Area: | 275 sq. mi. (712 sq km) |

# MICRONESIA

Micronesia is located in the Pacific Ocean and extends across the Caroline Island archipelago. The flag of Micronesia was adopted in 1978; it did not change in 1986 when the country gained independence. The design is based on the 1962 flag of the former United States Trust Territory of the Pacific Islands. In the Micronesian flag there are only four stars instead of the original six. They stand for the states of Yap, Pohnpei, Truk, and Kosrae. The color blue of the field is called "United Nations" blue because of its similarity in hue to the United Nations flag. Micronesia is an independent federated state, but is in free association with the United States.

| MICRONESIA | |
|---|---|
| Official Name: | Federated States of Micronesia |
| Capital: | Pohnpei |
| Languages: | English, Micronesian |
| Religions: | Roman Catholic, Protestant |
| Exports: | Fish, pepper, coconut meat, handcrafts |
| Imports: | Fuel, construction materials, transportation, foodstuffs |
| Highest Point: | 2,595 ft. (791 m) |
| Lowest Point: | Sea level |
| Area: | 217 sq. mi. (562 sq km) |

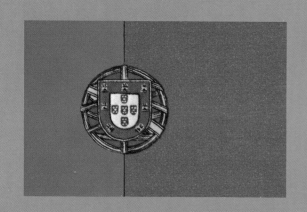

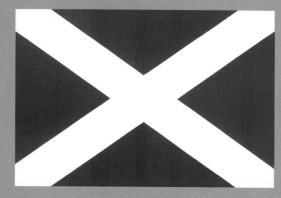

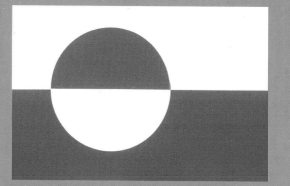

# CHAPTER FIVE

## *Europe*

At the time of this writing, almost every Western European nation has joined what is now called the European Community. This union will mean unencumbered travel and economic trade throughout Europe. There is movement toward a unified currency as well. The excitement that the European Community generates is, of course, great. Never before in the history of the world has such unification occurred peacefully on such a large scale. What military generals and dictators previously have attempted to accomplish by force has been peacefully accomplished by the desire of the European people. In the coming years, the European Community may well serve as an example not only for the rest of Europe, but also for the world at large.

What this means for Europe's national flags is uncertain. East and West Germany reunified in 1990 under the flag of West Germany. The Commonwealth of Independent States (formerly the Union of Soviet Socialist Republics) is also undergoing substantial changes, and, in all probability, the flags that some member nations have hoisted in the past will not be raised in the future.

The following pages offer the current national flags of a diverse continent that, at the present time, is home to some of the oldest national flags. What the future holds is as exciting as what the past has wrought.

## ICELAND

Iceland was an independent republic from A.D. 930 until 1262, under Norwegian rule from 1262 to 1380, and under Danish rule from 1380 until 1918. The national flag of Iceland was introduced in 1913, when the island was seeking home rule. The flag was made official in 1915, but could only be used in home waters, since the island was still under Danish rule. In 1918, when Iceland became a separate realm, the flag was made legal by King Christian X for all uses.

It is easy to see the influence of Norway's flag on that of Iceland, since Iceland's flag colors are the reverse of Norway's (see **Norway**). The blue and white are said to date back to ancient times; they are also the colors of the Order of the Silver Falcon. The red cross was added to acknowledge Iceland's association with Norway. By choosing a cross flag, Iceland acknowledged its status as a Scandinavian country.

Iceland's flag often appears in the swallowtail or *splitflag* form, like the flag of Denmark.

| ICELAND | |
|---|---|
| Official Name: | Republic of Iceland |
| Capital: | Reykjavik |
| Languages: | Icelandic |
| Religions: | Lutheran |
| Exports: | Fish and fish products, animal products |
| Imports: | Machinery, transportation equipment, petroleum, food |
| Highest Point: | 6,952 ft. (2,119 m) |
| Lowest Point: | Sea level |
| Area: | 39,769 sq. mi. (102,962 sq km) |

## IRELAND

Celtic tribes invaded Ireland four centuries before the birth of Christ. Their culture and literature flourished and spread to Scotland and elsewhere in the fifth century A.D., the same century that St. Patrick converted the Irish to Christianity.

The English began to invade Ireland in the twelfth century. Since that time, the Anglo-Irish struggle has continued with bitter rebellions and vicious reprisals of repression. From at least 1642, the traditional Irish flag was the green flag with a golden harp, used in the nationalist uprising of 1798 (often referred to as the "Year of Liberty"), even though the orange was then adopted by the loyalists to commemorate King William of Orange. This green flag with a golden harp served as the flag of Ireland until after the Easter Monday Rebellion of 1916, a nationalist uprising at which a tricolor that had been used by nationalists for eighty years was hoisted, along with other flags, in Dublin. The rebellion failed but was followed with guerrilla warfare and harsh response by British troops, the Black and Tans. Because of this uprising, the new flag became a national emblem.

In 1919, the Dáil Eireann (the Irish Parliament), in its first meeting, reaffirmed independence and, in 1921, England offered dominion status to six counties of Ulster and to the twenty-six counties of southern Ireland. The constitution of the Irish Free State, a British dominion, was adopted in December 1922. But Northern Ireland remained a part of the United Kingdom.

On December 29, 1937, a new constitution was adopted by a direct vote of the people, and it declared the name of the state to be Eire in the Irish language (Ireland in English) and declared Eire/Ireland a sovereign democratic state. In 1948, an Irish law made the country a republic instead of a dominion, so Ireland withdrew from the Commonwealth. In 1949, the British Parliament recognized both actions, but reasserted England's claim to the six north-

TOP: *The circle-cross, an ancient Celtic symbol.*

BOTTOM: *The United States' Stars and Stripes and Ireland's Tricolor.*

eastern counties of Ulster into the United Kingdom. This claim has not been recognized by Ireland, which favors peaceful unification of all of Ireland.

The national flag of Ireland, a vertical tricolor, has been in use by Irish nationalist organizations since at least 1848. Many believe the flag to have been inspired by the French Tricolor, a symbol of a successful democratic revolution. It is said that often both flags were flown side by side. In adopting the French Tricolor, the Irish substituted their own traditional colors: green, for the "Emerald Island"; orange, to recall the Protestant hero, King William of Orange, as well as the Ulsterman of the North; and white, for the hope for peace and unity on the island. The Irish tricolor came into use in 1921, with the birth of the Irish Free State. In 1937, when the Republic of Ireland finally achieved independence, the flag was adopted officially.

The display and design of the Irish national flag is governed by a set of rules closely based on the Flag Code of the United States of America.

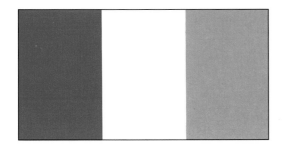

| IRELAND | |
|---|---|
| Official Name: | Republic of Ireland |
| Capital: | Dublin |
| Languages: | Irish Gaelic, English |
| Religions: | Roman Catholic, Anglican |
| Exports: | Meat and dairy products, textiles, machinery |
| Imports: | Petroleum, pet products, machinery |
| Highest Point: | 3,414 ft. (1,041 m) |
| Lowest Point: | Sea level |
| Area: | 27,136 sq. mi. (70,255 sq km) |

# UNITED KINGDOM

The United Kingdom is made up of four separate nations—English, Welsh, Scots, and the Irish of Northern Ireland. England and Scotland, originally separate kingdoms, united in 1707. Wales is a principality. Despite previous invasions, since 1066 England has been free of foreign invaders; consequently many British symbols are centuries old. In addition to the Union Jack and other national symbols, local flags and emblems are used by Scotland, Wales, and Northern Ireland. The United Kingdom also flies the Royal Standard, which is the personal flag of the British monarch. Each British dependency also hoists its own flag: however, dependencies' flags are usually a variation on the Union Flag of Britain.

## ENGLAND

The British Union Flag, the national flag of Great Britain, combines the crosses of St. George and St. Andrew, the traditional national flags of England and Scotland, respectively, with the saltire of St. Patrick.

Just how St. George's cross became a symbol of England is unknown. However, its use has been steeped in tradition since the thirteenth century and probably is derived from the Crusades. The first Union Flag was made in 1606, three years after King James VI of Scotland ascended to the throne of England as James I, thus uniting Scotland and England.

Since 1634, the Union Flag at sea has been reserved for use by the ships of the Royal Navy. In 1649 the union between England and Scotland was broken, and the Union Flag ceased to be used. Reestablished in 1658, the Union Flag bore in the center the blue shield of Ireland with a gold harp, but the flag lasted only two years, until the restoration of the monarchy. After England and Scotland reunited in 1654, a third Union Flag was adopted in 1658. This flag resembled the flag of 1606, but carried the Irish harp in its center. After the Irish harp was deleted in 1660, the Union Flag, confirmed in 1707, remained the same until 1801. At

this time a new flag was adopted, which combined the crosses of St. George and St. Andrew with the saltire of St. Patrick.

St. Patrick's cross, a red saltire on a white field, was an Irish symbol in the mid-fifteenth century. It was used as the personal arms and banner of the Fitzgeralds, the earls of Kildare. At the beginning of the seventeenth century, this flag was displayed at the Battle of Kinsale and in the seal granted to Trinity College, Dublin, and later came to be known as the banner of St. Patrick of Ireland. In 1783, St. Patrick's cross became the badge of the Knights of St. Patrick; seventeen years later it was introduced into the Union Flag as an emblem of Ireland, which fit conveniently with the crosses of St. Andrew and St. George. Those unfamiliar with this flag's early uses have sometimes challenged the authenticity of the St. Patrick's saltire.

In the United Kingdom, there is no set of written guidelines governing proper treatment of the Union Flag. It is equally unclear what constitutes misuse and what action could be brought against anyone who was judged to be misusing the flag. In England, the flag has been made into various items, such as jackets, umbrellas, hats, and bathing suits. None of this has brought reprisals. And if someone wishes to carry his or her packages in a bag made from the Union Flag, it is not only legal but socially acceptable; such behavior is interpreted as meaning that the national flag is a source of happiness and pride for its user.

| UNITED KINGDOM | |
|---|---|
| Official Name: | United Kingdom of Great Britain and Northern Ireland |
| Capital: | London |
| Languages: | English |
| Religions: | Anglican, Roman Catholic, Presbyterian |
| Exports: | Machinery, transportation equipment, petroleum |
| Imports: | Machinery, food, crude materials |
| Highest Point: | 4,406 ft. (1,343 m) |
| Lowest Point: | -9 ft. (-3 m) |
| Area: | 94,092 sq. mi. (243,604 sq km) |

ENGLAND; NATIONAL FLAG SINCE AT LEAST 1277

UNITED KINGDOM; STATE FLAG 1707–1800

UNITED KINGDOM; CURRENT FLAG

LEFT: *The Tower Bridge is often confused with the London Bridge in Great Britain's capital.*

OPPOSITE: *"Big Ben" is part of the Houses of Parliament in London.*

© Steve Vidler/Leo de Wys, Inc.

## The Union Flag/Union Jack Controversy

The Union Flag is often referred to as the "Union Jack." The term "Jack" originally referred only to the Union Flag when a vessel of the Royal Navy flies it at the jackstaff, that is, the flagstaff at the bow. Just where "Jack" originated is not clear. One theory suggests that "Jack" is an anglicized version of the Latin or French forms of James: Jacobus or Jacques. Another more popular theory is that "Jack" dates back to the 1640s and the days of the Stuart kings, when it was decreed that royal vessels must fly a jack (by then, a naval colloquialism for a small flag) at the bow.

## The Royal Standard

In this century, the Royal Standard has been the personal banner of the monarch of Britain. Previously, it served as the "arms of dominion." At first, these "arms of dominion" represented only England, as in the standard of Richard I (1189–1199), which displayed the now-famous three gold lions on a red field. During Edward III's

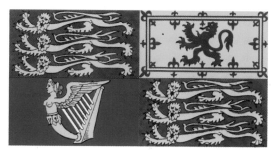

**ROYAL STANDARD**

reign (1327–1377), he demonstrated his claim to the throne of France by adding the French arms, the fleurs-de-lis (lilies), to his standard. In 1603 when James VI of Scotland became King James I of England, the Royal Standard showed the arms of England in the first and fourth quarters, and Scotland and Ireland in the second and third quarters respectively. Under the Hanoverian monarchs of the eighteenth and early nineteenth centuries, the arms of Hanover appeared in the fourth quarter or in the center of the Royal Standard. When King George III renounced his claim to the throne of France, the French fleurs-de-lis were omitted from the British standard after four and a half centuries of use. The arms of England filled the first and fourth quarters, Scotland the second, and Ireland the third. When Queen Victoria ascended to the throne in 1837, she removed the Hanoverian arms, made some minor alterations, and the Royal Standard took its present form. Wales has never been represented on the Royal Standard.

When the Royal Standard is hoisted over Westminster Abbey, it means that the monarch is within the Abbey itself or in its vicinity. When flown at a vessel's masthead, it signifies that the monarch is on board.

The queen has another flag that she uses in countries that are not a part of the Commonwealth, and therefore, not under the "Queen's Realms." This flag contains her crowned initial 'E' set within a golden chaplet.

The other members of the royal family have their own personal standards, too. For example, Prince Charles's personal flag, for use during his visits to Wales, centers his symbol, the coronet, against a green shield on the Standard of Wales.

## Ensigns

At sea, the British use a form of the national flag called the Red Ensign. This flag was originally adopted in 1625 and bore the cross of either St. George or St. Andrew in the canton. In 1707, the flag changed to the original form of the Union Flag, and later, in 1801, was replaced by the present flag.

The Blue Ensign has been reserved for government vessels since 1864. This flag often carries an official badge in the fly and, combined with the local arms or emblem, forms the government flag of the British dependencies. Bermuda is the only dependency with the right to display its arms on the Red Ensign for use on land as a national flag.

Like the Blue Ensign, the White Ensign has been reserved for use by the Royal Navy since 1864.

*ABOVE: Hot-air ballooning is popular in Britain.*

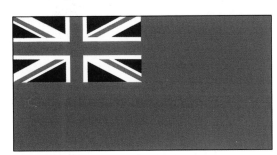

ENGLAND; RED ENSIGN

## WALES

Wales's history began in a sense when early Anglo-Saxon tribes drove Celtic peoples into the mountains of Wales, calling them *Waelise* ("Welsh," or "foreign"), thus helping to create a distinct nationality. In 1301, Edward of Caernarvon, son of Edward I, became the first Prince of Wales.

*RIGHT: Technically, the royal arms may be used only by the Queen and her government.*

Wales is considered a principality of England. The flag of Wales is derived from a flag from the Tudor period during the late 1400s. The dynastic colors of the Tudors, white and green, form the background of the flag, which has been in use since at least 1911. The traditional Red Dragon of Wales is associated with the legendary King Arthur.

*ABOVE: Medieval reenactment groups such as the Plantagenet Society use heraldic banners.*

*RIGHT: The Union Jack is popular as part of clothing and accessory items in Britain.*

*BELOW: Stonehenge, thousands of years old, originally served religious purposes.*

## SCOTLAND

Scotland's flag is known as the saltire, or cross of St. Andrew. This symbol, probably as well known, if not more so than the cross of St. George, has two legends attached to it. The first involves St. Andrew who, when condemned to a martyr's death, felt himself unworthy to suffer in the exact manner as Christ, and was crucified instead on two diagonal beams. Some time later, when his remains were being transported, the ship on which they were being carried was shipwrecked: His relics were beached along Scotland's coast, where they were revered. The second legend involves Scottish King Achaius, who saw a diagonal cross in the sky and adopted it as his national emblem.

On land, the saltire is often illegally replaced by the Scottish Red Lion, which also forms the fourth canton in the Royal Standard.

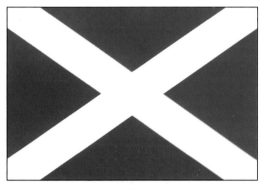

SCOTLAND; NATIONAL FLAG SINCE THE THIRTEENTH CENTURY

## NORTHERN IRELAND

Northern Ireland has used the Union Flag as its official flag since the imposition of direct rule by Britain in 1972. However, from 1924 until 1972, the flag was a banner of the arms of the Northern Irish government.

TOP: Scotland has many famous buildings, including Stirling Castle, shown here.

RIGHT: Edinburgh Castle is in the capital city of Scotland, now a part of the United Kingdom.

# NORWAY

Norway as a nation dates back to A.D. 872, when its first supreme ruler, Harald the Fairheaded, came to power. However, the national flag, designed in 1821, is based on the flag of Denmark, to which Norway (as well as Iceland) once belonged. That year, the Parliament laid a blue cross over the Danish cross, an idea derived from the colors of the French Tricolor. In the 1800s, the Norwegian flag bore an emblem, the combined crosses of Norway and Sweden, to represent Norway's link to Sweden. In 1899, the emblem was removed from Norway's flag, leading to the dissolution of the union between the two countries in 1905, and to Norway's subsequent independence, with its own flag and king. The king's personal flag of a crowned rampant lion holding the golden ax of St. Olaf against a red field was adopted as the Royal Standard.

The Norwegian flag, with its red, white, and blue colors, served as inspiration for the flags of Iceland and the Faroe Islands and came to be known as the "Norse colors." The Norwegian flag was also the first flag at the South Pole, reached by Captain Roald Amundsen on December 14, 1911. This fifty-five-day trek was accomplished by Captain Amundsen and his four-member crew on skis and dogsleds. The group embedded the Norwegian flag in the ice and thirty days later, when Captain Robert Scott, Amundsen's British rival, arrived at the South Pole, the flag was still there.

| NORWAY | |
|---|---|
| Official Name: | Kingdom of Norway |
| Capital: | Oslo |
| Languages: | Norwegian, Lapp |
| Religions: | Lutheran |
| Exports: | Petroleum, natural gas, metals, paper |
| Imports: | Machinery, transportation equipment, food, iron |
| Highest Point: | 8,110 ft. (2,472 m) |
| Lowest Point: | Sea level |
| Area: | 149,158 sq. mi. (386,170 sq km) |

*BELOW: The ancient merchant city of Bergen, Norway, is still a thriving port.*

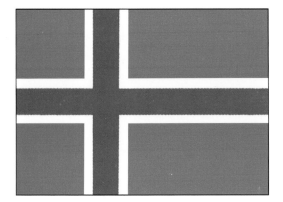

## SWEDEN

Sweden, home to its people for at least five thousand years, is the oldest stable European community and derives its flag from its basic arms, three gold crowns on blue. The flag dates back to A.D. 1523, when King Gustavus I Vasa ascended to the throne. From 1844 through 1906, the Swedish flag's canton carried the emblem of the Swedish-Norwegian union.

Like Denmark's flag, Sweden's flag has a swallowtail version reserved for state use. However, Sweden's swallowtail has a pointed tongue that extends the yellow Scandinavian cross.

Stockholm is the business, cultural, and governmental center of Sweden.

| SWEDEN | |
|---|---|
| Official Name: | Kingdom of Sweden |
| Capital: | Stockholm |
| Languages: | Swedish |
| Religions: | Lutheran |
| Exports: | Machinery, motor vehicles, wood pulp |
| Imports: | Machinery, petroleum, chemicals, food |
| Highest Point: | 6,926 ft. (2,111 m) |
| Lowest Point: | Sea level |
| Area: | 173,780 sq. mi. (449,916 sq km) |

## SCANIA

Scania is in southern Sweden. This region was under Danish control until 1658 and has struggled for many years for self-government. Its flag, a red field bearing the yellow Scandinavian cross, is well known throughout Sweden and derives its colors from both Denmark and Sweden.

## FINLAND

Finland was a part of Sweden from 1157 until 1809, when it became a part of the Russian Empire. Nevertheless, Finland maintained a strong national spirit and in 1917 declared its independence. Because its heraldic colors are red and yellow, several flags during Finland's independence movement were made in these two colors—even a banner used during Finland's one-year civil war, which began in 1917. However, in May of 1918, due to popular demand, Finland adopted a national flag whose color combination (a blue Scandinavian cross [see **Denmark**] on a white field) had been first used in 1862 on separatist banners against Russia. The flag's colors represent Finland's blue lakes and its white snowfields.

| FINLAND | |
|---|---|
| Official Name: | Republic of Finland |
| Capital: | Helsinki |
| Languages: | Finnish, Swedish |
| Religions: | Lutheran, Greek Orthodox |
| Exports: | Wood, paper and wood pulp, machinery |
| Imports: | Fuels, chemicals, machinery, food |
| Highest Point: | 4,357 ft. (1,328 m) |
| Lowest Point: | Sea level |
| Area: | 130,558 sq. mi. (338,015 sq km) |

## *ALAND ISLANDS*

The Aland Islands are an autonomous Finnish island group in the Baltic Sea. In 1809, the islands, considered part of Finland, were ceded to Russia. In 1921, the islands were granted self-government. The flag, created the same year, remained unofficial until 1954. The flag can only be used on land.

*Tivoli Park in Copenhagen is a world-famous amusement center.*

# DENMARK

The kingdom of Denmark dates back to ancient times and the Danish cross flag, called the *Dannebrog* (literally "Danish cloth," or figuratively, the "strength of Denmark"), is one of the oldest flags in use today.

The original flag was square with an equal-armed cross (similar to the cross of St. George—see **United Kingdom**), which first appeared on the royal arms of King Valdemar IV Atterdag (1340–1375); however, according to folk legend, during the Battle of Lyndanisse in 1219, in which the Christian Danes were victorious over the pagan Estonians, the flag appeared as a vision to the Danes and fell from heaven.

Over time, the equal-armed cross extended into what is now known as the Scandinavian cross. The red and white color was a common color choice for flags in Christian Europe at the time the Danish adopted their flag. The Scandinavian cross and flag design spread to other Scandinavian nations and to Germany, and is still a reminder of the time when the Danes colonized Europe.

The people of Denmark proudly display their *Dannebrog* whenever possible: The flag is used in many different settings, including town halls, gardens, office buildings, and even on Christmas trees. Children often paint their faces in its design, which also often adorns many other items, even beer cans.

| | DENMARK |
|---|---|
| Official Name: | Kingdom of Denmark |
| Capital: | Copenhagen |
| Languages: | Danish |
| Religions: | Lutheran |
| Exports: | Meat and dairy products, machinery, textiles |
| Imports: | Raw materials, fuels, machinery, transportation equipment |
| Highest Point: | 568 ft. (173 m) |
| Lowest Point: | -23 ft. (-7 m) |
| Area: | 16,633 sq. mi. (43,063 sq km) |

## *GREENLAND*

Greenland, a large polar wasteland located mostly within the Arctic Circle, is a Danish dependency. In 1979, Greenland won home rule and since that time, Eskimo political parties have dominated the Landsting, the local parliament. Also in 1979, the island conducted a competition to find a flag of local design; finally, in 1985 an agreement was reached. The present flag, which represents the sun rising over the polar ice, is used on land and at sea.

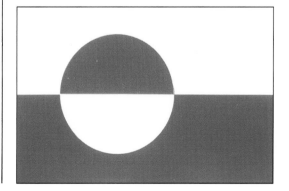

| | GREENLAND |
|---|---|
| Official Name: | Greenland |
| Capital: | Godthaab |
| Languages: | Danish, indigenous |
| Religions: | Lutheran |
| Exports: | Fish and fish products, metallic ores |
| Imports: | Petroleum, machinery, transportation equipment, food |
| Highest Point: | 12,139 ft. (3,700 m) |
| Lowest Point: | Sea level |
| Area: | 840,004 sq. mi. (2,174,770 sq km) |

## *FAROE ISLANDS*

The Faroe Islands, a dependency of Denmark, are located in the North Atlantic Ocean. In the 1900s, a self-government movement began, although the local parliament, or Lagting, had been reinstated by Denmark in 1852. The present flag, inspired by the flag of Iceland (see **Iceland**), was designed by several Faroese students in 1919. The Scandinavian cross and the three colors express unity with the rest of Scandinavia. The flag was made semi-official in 1931; in 1940, it became official for use at sea; and in 1948, it was allowed for all uses. The present shade of blue was adopted in 1959.

## LUXEMBOURG

Luxembourg was created as a county of the Netherlands in A.D. 963. During the 1300s, Luxembourg became a duchy. In 1795, France seized control of the area and ruled until 1815, when Luxembourg became a realm of the Dutch royal house. After Belgium separated from the Netherlands, Luxembourg became a grand duchy in 1839. It became an independent and neutral state in 1867, although the king of the Netherlands was still its ruler until 1890.

The tricolor flag, although resembling the Dutch flag, developed quite independently. The three colors can be found on the country's traditional arms, which date back at least to 1247 and the reign of Count Henry VI. The flag was first used in 1815. Recognition was given to the tricolor in 1845 and again in 1923 and 1972. Although the design is the same as the flag of the Netherlands, the shade of blue is not quite so dark. Moreover, the historical origin of each flag is quite distinct.

The latest specifications permit the national flag to be in proportions of either 1:2 or 2:3.

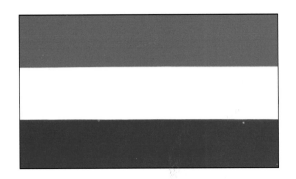

| LUXEMBOURG | |
|---|---|
| Official Name: | Grand Duchy of Luxembourg |
| Capital: | Luxembourg |
| Languages: | Luxembourgish, French, German |
| Religions: | Roman Catholic |
| Exports: | Steel, plastic, rubber products |
| Imports: | Coal, petroleum, consumer goods |
| Highest Point: | 1,834 ft. (559 m) |
| Lowest Point: | 427 ft. (130 m) |
| Area: | 998 sq. mi. (2,584 sq km) |

## THE NETHERLANDS

In 1815, the Congress of Vienna formed the Kingdom of the Netherlands (which at that time included Belgium) under William I. In 1830, Belgium seceded and formed a separate country (see **Belgium**).

The Dutch tricolor is one of the earliest national flags in the modern sense of the word. The flag itself dates back to the 1500s, when the inhabitants of the Netherlands fought for their independence from Spain. At the time, the tricolor's upper stripe was orange, taken from the arms of William the Silent, Prince of Orange. This flag came to be known as the *Prinsenvlag*; the orange is now the dynastic color of the ruling house of the Netherlands. The flag's orange stripe was changed to red around 1630, reflecting the formation and color of the republic, the Dutch States-General.

Except from 1810 to 1813, when the country was part of France, the simple red-white-blue tricolor has always flown over the Netherlands. Nevertheless the Batavian Republic of 1796–1807 added—for the

*Despite one of the world's highest population concentrations, the Netherlands has many pleasant urban parks.*

naval ensign only—a special white canton with a female figure symbolizing liberty. The flag was made official in 1937, including its proportions and colors (specified as vermilion red and cobalt blue). All Dutch cities and towns hoist their own flags, on which the rampant lion of Holland is often displayed.

| THE NETHERLANDS | |
|---|---|
| Official Name: | Kingdom of the Netherlands |
| Capital: | Amsterdam |
| Languages: | Dutch |
| Religions: | Roman Catholic, Protestant |
| Exports: | Food, machinery, chemicals, petroleum |
| Imports: | Machinery, petroleum, transportation equipment |
| Highest Point: | 1,053 ft. (321 m) |
| Lowest Point: | -22 ft. (-7 m) |
| Area: | 15,892 sq. mi. (41,144 sq km) |

*LEFT: Wooden shoes were developed for walking in the marshy soil of the Netherlands.*

# BELGIUM

Belgium, once a part of the Netherlands, became an independent monarchy in 1830. The Belgian colors were first used in the Belgians' rising against the Austrians, over whom they were victorious in 1789. From 1792 until 1814, Belgium was dominated by France; from 1814 until 1830, Belgium was a part of the Netherlands. During these years of foreign rule, the Belgium colors were used by those who fought for independence. At first, the tricolor was horizontal, but after independence in 1830, the government decreed that the flag would be vertical to resemble the French Tricolor. The black, yellow, and red colors of the Belgian flag are the principal colors of the arms of Brabant. The flag for use on land has the unusual proportions of 13:15.

*BELOW: An eighteenth-century ship sailing in the port of Antwerp.*

*BELOW: The famous Dutch tulip actually originated in Turkey.*

| | BELGIUM |
|---|---|
| Official Name: | Kingdom of Belgium |
| Capital: | Brussels |
| Languages: | Dutch, French, German |
| Religions: | Roman Catholic |
| Exports: | Machinery, chemicals, food, livestock |
| Imports: | Machinery, fuels, food, motor vehicles |
| Highest Point: | 2,277 ft. (694 m) |
| Lowest Point: | Sea level |
| Area: | 11,783 sq. mi. (30,506 sq km) |

# GERMANY

Germany has two rich and distinct flag traditions. Each tradition is based on separate color combinations and within these, many flags can be found in a myriad of forms.

The present black, red, and gold are the oldest of Germany's flag colors. The use of these colors dates back to the start of the Napoleonic Wars, before Germany was a united country. The colors originated from the 1813 uniforms worn by troops of the Lutzow Freikorps regiment; these were black and red with gold decorations.

The black, red, and gold tricolor was used during the first all-German parliament (1848–1850). Later, in 1867, the use of the tricolor was replaced by a flag of black, white, and red, designed by Bismarck, who, in 1871, was responsible for unifying the German states into an empire. This flag continued to be used by German nationalists even after the establishment of the first republic in 1919, which officially adopted the black, red, and gold colors. When Adolf Hitler rose to power in 1933, like Bismarck, he adopted a black, white, and red flag. At the same time, the swastika flag of the Nazi party was made an equal national flag and two years later the black-white-red tricolor was abandoned. The red of the Nazi flag was said to stand for socialism, the white central disk for nationalism. The swastika (previously widely used by traditional societies around the world) was chosen as an Aryan symbol for Hitler's racist regime.

In 1945, after the Nazis were defeated, the divided German states returned to the use of the black, red, and gold flag. In 1949, West Germany officially adopted this tricolor, as did East Germany, although in 1959 the latter also placed its state emblem in the flag's center. This emblem was a communist symbol and depicted a hammer (which represented heavy industry), a protractor (scientific progress), and a wreath of wheat ears (agriculture).

In October 1990, Germany reunified after forty-five years of separation, and the black-red-gold tricolor used by West Germany continued for the reunited country as the national flag. Marking the country's rebirth, a twenty-by-thirty-three-foot (6-by-10-m) tricolor was hoisted before the Reichstag in the exact spot where the first German republic was declared in 1918.

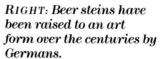

| | GERMANY | |
|---|---|---|
| Official Name: | Federal Republic of Germany | |
| Capital: | Berlin | |
| Languages: | German | |
| Religions: | Roman Catholic, Protestant | |
| Exports: | Machinery, chemical products, textiles, motor vehicles, iron | |
| Imports: | Raw materials, machinery, fuels, manufactured goods | |
| Highest Point: | 9,721 ft. (2,263 m) | |
| Lowest Point: | -7 ft. (-2 m) | |
| Area: | 137,787 sq. mi. (356,731 sq km) | |

*RIGHT: Beer steins have been raised to an art form over the centuries by Germans.*

GERMAN CONFEDERATION; WAR ENSIGN 1848–1852

KINGDOM OF PRUSSIA; WAR ENSIGN 1858–1863

*ABOVE: Neuschwanstein Castle in Bavaria was built in the nineteenth century.*

**GERMAN EMPIRE; WAR ENSIGN 1903–1921**

**GERMAN REICH; NATIONAL FLAG 1935–1945**

© W. Hille/Leo de Wys, Inc.

*BELOW: The fall of the Berlin Wall and the unification of the divided city gave Germans great joy in 1990.*

© Associated Press/Wide World Photos

*ABOVE: The typical German Farben is a long vertically hung flag.*

*RIGHT: Frankfurt is Germany's thriving commercial and communications center.*

© Casimir/Leo de Wys, Inc.

# POLAND

Poland's flag is prototypical of a livery-colored flag and uses the two main colors of the country's shield of arms. The arms, with a crowned eagle, date back to 1228. In 1241, the red and white colors were used on the arms and by the Kingdom of Poland until 1795, when the kingdom was abolished and Poland was partitioned. The new republic (1918–39) again took up the arms and in 1927 the shield gained a gold border. After the Second World War the Polish People's Republic was established and the crown was omitted from the head of the eagle in the coat of arms. In 1990, after the fall of communism in Poland, the crown was restored. The Polish shield appears in the center of the white stripe of the national flag for use by merchant ships, the diplomatic service, and airports.

| POLAND | |
|---|---|
| Official Name: | Republic of Poland |
| Capital: | Warsaw |
| Languages: | Polish |
| Religions: | Roman Catholic |
| Exports: | Machinery, equipment, fuels, manufactured goods |
| Imports: | Machinery, petroleum, raw materials |
| Highest Point: | 8,199 ft. (2,499 m) |
| Lowest Point: | -6 ft. (-2 m) |
| Area: | 120,728 sq. mi. (312,565 sq km) |

# CZECHOSLOVAKIA

In 1848, Slovakia unofficially adopted the pan-Slavic colors of white, blue, and red used by Imperial Russia. With its formation in 1918, the republic of Czechoslovakia was able to choose a flag of its own. After several designs were discussed, the present tricolor was adopted in 1920. This flag allots equal space to the red and white of Bohemia-Moravia (Czech lands) and to the white, blue, and red of Slovakia. Despite the fact that the flag was suppressed during German occupation, it was restored in 1945 with the liberation of the country and has remained in use since that time.

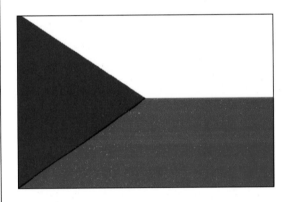

| CZECHOSLOVAKIA | |
|---|---|
| Official Name: | Czech and Slovak Federal Republic |
| Capital: | Prague |
| Languages: | Czech, Slovak, Hungarian |
| Religions: | Roman Catholic, Protestant, Greek Orthodox |
| Exports: | Machinery, transportation equipment, iron, steel |
| Imports: | Fuels, machinery, raw materials, transportation equipment |
| Highest Point: | 8,737 ft. (2,663 m) |
| Lowest Point: | 308 ft. (94 m) |
| Area: | 49,381 sq. mi. (127,847 sq km) |

# HUNGARY

Hungary's tricolor flag uses the same colors as the country's coat of arms, which is divided horizontally. One version of the arms is known as the "Kossuth" arms, after the national hero who formed the Free State in 1849. It was at this same time that the flag's form, inspired by the Tricolor of France, was adopted. Until 1945, the Hungarian flag bore the crown of St. Stephen with its characteristic bent cross. In 1949, and until the revolt of 1956, a Soviet-styled emblem was used at the center of the flag. At the present time, no emblem adorns the flag.

| HUNGARY | |
|---|---|
| Official Name: | Republic of Hungary |
| Capital: | Budapest |
| Languages: | Hungarian |
| Religions: | Roman Catholic, Calvinist, Lutheran |
| Exports: | Machinery, transportation equipment, agricultural produce |
| Imports: | Machinery, transportation equipment, fuels, chemicals |
| Highest Point: | 3,330 ft. (1,015 m) |
| Lowest Point: | 259 ft. (79 m) |
| Area: | 35,921 sq. mi. (92,999 sq km) |

# ROMANIA

The complex political history of Romania is reflected in the diversity of flags it has had. In 1834 Turkish authorities granted the principalities of Moldavia and Walachia flags of their own for limited use—blue with a white ox head and yellow with a white bird, respectively, each with a red canton bearing three white stars. The Paris Convention of 1858 recognized the United Principalities of Moldavia and Walachia, which displayed a horizontal tricolor of red-yellow-blue. The flag dates back to the vertical tricolor of blue-yellow-red, inspired by the French flag during the revolutionary events in both countries in 1848. That flag was reestablished in 1867 and different changes were made in the central coat of arms in the following decades. In 1866 the name of the country was changed to Romania.

In 1948, four months after a communist republic was formed, the arms of the People's Republic became the official flag emblem. This depicted the country's forests and mountains, with an oil derrick and the rising sun. Since then, there have been several alterations; the last form dates back to 1965.

In 1989 Communist dictator Nicolae Ceausescu was deposed and executed. While revolutionaries cut the Communist coat of arms from the center of the flag, as an official design there was established the simple blue-yellow-red tricolor first used in 1848.

*Opposition to communism in Romania was expressed by cutting communist symbols from the national flag.*

| ROMANIA | |
|---|---|
| Official Name: | Romania |
| Capital: | Bucharest |
| Languages: | Romanian |
| Religions: | Romanian Orthodox, Roman Catholic |
| Exports: | Machinery, fuels, textiles, wood |
| Imports: | Machinery, fuels, iron ore, motor vehicles |
| Highest Point: | 8,343 ft. (2,543 m) |
| Lowest Point: | Sea level |
| Area: | 91,699 sq. mi. (237,409 sq km) |

# BULGARIA

Bulgaria had no national flag before its liberation war in 1878. The following year it adopted the Russian tricolor out of gratitude for the help rendered by Russia against the Turks. A change was made, however; the central stripe was altered from blue to green. After the Communists came to power in 1947 they added a coat of arms in the white stripe near the hoist. This particular version depicted a rampant lion (a component of the Bulgarian arms since 1879) with a pale blue background and a red star (representing communism) above it. Three different versions were introduced over the course of the years. All of them had a cogwheel symbolizing industrialization and the 1971 version included the dates 681 (the foundation of Bulgaria) and 1944 (formation of the Communist government.)

On November 27, 1990, Bulgaria modified its flag again, removing the coat of arms from the white, green, and red tricolor.

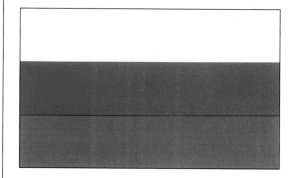

| BULGARIA | |
|---|---|
| Official Name: | Republic of Bulgaria |
| Capital: | Sofia |
| Languages: | Bulgarian |
| Religions: | Bulgarian Orthodox, Muslim |
| Exports: | Machinery, agricultural products, fuels |
| Imports: | Fuels, machinery, transportation equipment |
| Highest Point: | 9,596 ft. (2,925 m) |
| Lowest Point: | Sea level |
| Area: | 42,823 sq. mi. (110,869 sq km) |

# GREECE

The accomplishments of the ancient Greeks in architecture, science, art, mathematics, drama, philosophy, literature, and democracy are thriving legacies.

In ancient times, Greece did not use flags, except for a red signal displayed on ships during warfare.

From 1453 until 1821, Greece was a part of the Ottoman Empire and used its flags like many of the other countries under Turkish rule. In 1821, Greece began a war of independence from Turkey that lasted until 1829. Greece became a republic in 1924, but the monarchy was restored in 1935. After many different kinds of government, today Greece has a republican government.

The white and blue of the current Greek flag are the colors of an earlier flag and coincidentally are the colors of Bavaria, the country of origin of George II, who became the first king of Greece in 1832. The canton with the cross was once the original flag; the blue stripes are thought to represent the nine syllables of the Greek motto, which translates as "Liberty or Death." The design was most probably inspired by the United States' Stars and Stripes.

Until 1970, the cross flag was usually flown on land, while the striped flag with the cross in the canton was used at sea and for seaports. In this way, Greece had two national flags until 1970, when the plain cross version was discontinued. In 1975, both flags were used again, and the plain cross was adopted as the national flag. In 1978, reflecting yet another political change in the Greek government, the striped flag was re-adopted as the national flag.

*TOP, RIGHT: The Acropolis is one of the early Greeks' many architectural accomplishments.*

© FPG International

| GREECE | |
|---|---|
| Official Name: | Hellenic Republic |
| Capital: | Athens |
| Languages: | Greek |
| Religions: | Greek Orthodox, Muslim |
| Exports: | Textiles, fruits, minerals |
| Imports: | Machinery, transportation equipment, petroleum |
| Highest Point: | 9,570 ft. (2,917 m) |
| Lowest Point: | Sea level |
| Area: | 50,944 sq. mi. (131,894 sq km) |

# ALBANIA

Albania was, for several centuries, a part of the Byzantine Empire, which used an emblem of a double-headed eagle. In the mid-1400s, the national hero George Castriota, or Skanderbeg, used the emblem when resisting the Turks of the Ottoman Empire. In 1478, Albania was annexed to Turkey until 1912, when Albania proclaimed its independence under the flag of Skanderbeg. Throughout 1914 and the reign of William of Wied, the double eagle carried lightning bolts in its claws and a white star was placed over its head; however, once William of Wied's reign was over in 1915, those symbols were omitted.

From 1939 to 1942, the eagle, which symbolizes rule over the East and West, was surrounded by Italian and fascist emblems, but even before Albania was liberated, these emblems were omitted. In 1945, the yellow-edged, five-pointed red star of communism was placed above the eagle's head. This version was confirmed in 1946, on the date of the National Anti-Fascist Congress.

| ALBANIA | |
|---|---|
| Official Name: | Republic of Albania |
| Capital: | Tiranë |
| Languages: | Albanian, Greek |
| Religions: | Muslim, Albanian Orthodox, Roman Catholic |
| Exports: | Asphalt, bitumen, petroleum products |
| Imports: | Machinery, machine tools, iron, steel |
| Highest Point: | 9,026 ft. (2,751 m) |
| Lowest Point: | Sea level |
| Area: | 11,100 sq. mi. (28,738 sq km) |

## *YUGOSLAVIA*

Serbia used the pan-Slavic colors of red, blue, and white as an acknowledgment of Russia's assistance in its fight for independence. After World War I, when the Austro-Hungarian Empire collapsed, the Kingdom of the Serbs, Croats, and the Slovenes was formed from the former provinces of Dalmatia, Bosnia, Croatia, Herzegovina, Slovenia, Voyvodina, and the independent states of Montenegro and Serbia. In 1929, this group of states came to be called Yugoslavia. In 1941, when Yugoslavia became a federal republic, Marshal Tito added the five-pointed red star of the Communist party and changed the flag's proportions from 2:3 to its present 1:2. In 1946, the star was enlarged, given a yellow border, and is now referred to as the "Partisan Star."

In 1991 Yugoslavia faced secession by Slovenia and Croatia, whose independence was recognized in January 1992 by European powers. Kosovo, Bosnia-Herzegovina, and Macedonia subsequently proclaimed their independence. Serbia and Montenegro, operating under the name and flag of Yugoslavia, tried to prevent the dismemberment of the state—or at least retain under their control areas with Serbian populations.

| YUGOSLAVIA | |
|---|---|
| Official Name: | Federal Republic of Yugoslavia |
| Capital: | Belgrade |
| Languages: | Serbo-Croatian, Slovene, Macedonian |
| Religions: | Serbian Orthodox, Roman Catholic, Muslim |
| Exports: | Food, leather goods and shoes, textiles |
| Imports: | Machinery, petroleum, iron and steel |
| Highest Point: | 9,396 ft. (2,864 m) |
| Lowest Point: | Sea level |
| Area: | 98,766 sq. mi. (255,705 sq km) |

## *CROATIA*

When the Slavic peoples of Eastern Europe rose in revolt against non-Slavic rulers in 1848, the Croatians chose red-white-blue as their national colors. The checkerboard coat of arms is said to date back centuries before that, but the crown over those arms was adopted only in late 1990. It consists of five historical shields—those of old Croatia, Dubrovnik, Dalmatia, Istria, and Slavonia.

| CROATIA | |
|---|---|
| Official Name: | Republic of Croatia |
| Capital: | Zagreb |
| Languages: | Croatian, Serbian |
| Religions: | Roman Catholic, Serbian Orthodox |
| Exports: | Oil, grains, shipbuilding materials |
| Imports: | Electronics |
| Highest Point: | 5,768 ft. (1,758 m) |
| Lowest Point: | Sea level |
| Area: | 21,829 sq. mi. (56,537 sq km) |

## *SLOVENIA*

The old coat of arms of the Austro-Hungarian province of Carniola included the colors white, blue, and red now incorporated in the Slovenian flag. These are recognized as a pan-Slavic symbol. The present flag was adopted in 1991 when independence was proclaimed. To distinguish it from the similar flags of Russia and Slovakia, Slovenia added its new coat of arms in the upper hoist. It represents the Alps and Adriatic coast with stars for the former Duchy of Celje.

| SLOVENIA | |
|---|---|
| Official Name: | Republic of Slovenia |
| Capital: | Ljubljana |
| Languages: | Slovene |
| Religions: | Roman Catholic |
| Exports: | Furniture, crystal, glass, shoes, toys, textiles |
| Imports: | Fuel, airplane parts, wheat, corn, leather |
| Highest Point: | 9,396 ft. (2,864 m) |
| Lowest Point: | Sea level |
| Area: | 7,819 sq. mi. (20,251 sq km) |

# ITALY

For centuries Italy was only a geographical term. The peninsula was divided into separate states, some of them independent and others controlled by the Catholic Church or other European powers. At that time, each state had its own heraldry and flag, and there was no attempt to unify the states until the late 1700s. Napoleon invaded Italy in 1796; it was during this period of upheaval that the colors of Italy were established. Influenced by the French Tricolor, the Italian tricolor was originally horizontal in form.

The green-white-red Italian colors date from 1796 and took their final form in 1798. The vertical stripes were used until 1802 when the same colors were arranged in a different form. The tricolor appeared again in 1848, the "Year of Revolutions," and later was adopted as the flag of the new Kingdom of Italy, which was created in 1861, after Italy was unified by Garibaldi in the movement known as the Risorgimento, or the Resurgence. At that time, a coat of arms adorned the center of the tricolor. With the termination of the kingdom in 1946, the arms were removed from the flag. At this point, the Italian national flag became the plain vertical tricolor, which carries the colors of the Milanese militia, green (like Muhammad, Napoleon is said to have favored the color green) and white.

The Italian flag, when at sea, is used with two different emblems at its center to distinguish the flag from the national flag of Mexico, which it closely resembles.

| **ITALY** | |
|---|---|
| Official Name: | Italian Republic |
| Capital: | Rome |
| Languages: | Italian |
| Religions: | Roman Catholic |
| Exports: | Machinery, transportation equipment |
| Imports: | Machinery, transportation equipment, food |
| Highest Point: | 15,771 ft. (4,807 m) |
| Lowest Point: | Sea level |
| Area: | 116,319 sq. mi. (301,150 sq km) |

*LEFT: The Leaning Tower in Pisa, Italy.*

© Steve Vidler/Leo de Wys, Inc.

*BELOW: The Cathedral overshadows other buildings in Florence, Italy.*

© Steve Vidler/Leo de Wys, Inc.

# SAN MARINO

San Marino is located in north central Italy, on the slopes of Mount Titano. This tiny sovereign nation was founded in the fourth century and claims to be the oldest state in Europe. San Marino's flag dates back at least to 1797, two years before Napoleon recognized the country's independence. The everyday flag is a simple white and eggshell blue; however, on official occasions, the arms, the source of the flag's colors, are placed in the flag's center.

| SAN MARINO | |
|---|---|
| Official Name: | Most Serene Republic of San Marino |
| Capital: | San Marino |
| Languages: | Italian |
| Religions: | Roman Catholic |
| Exports: | Construction materials, textiles, wine |
| Imports: | Consumer goods, petroleum, gold |
| Highest Point: | 2,425 ft. (739 m) |
| Lowest Point: | 174 ft. (53 m) |
| Area: | 24 sq. mi. (62 sq km) |

# MALTA

Malta was controlled by the Knights of the Order of St. John of Jerusalem from 1630 to 1798. This ancient order used a white cross against a red field.

In 1798, the country was seized by Napoleon, but by 1814, Malta was ceded to the British. There is some indication that the Maltese cross was displayed in red on a white flag (or with colors reversed) under the early years of British rule. Later, the traditional island flag of white and red vertical stripes, said to date back to the eleventh century, came into use. The people of Malta displayed great heroism during World War II and King George VI granted them the George Cross in 1943. This was represented the following year on a blue canton added to the white-red flag. Four years later, they hoisted a flag bearing these arms. In 1964, when Malta gained independence from Britain, it kept the George Cross but deleted the blue background to the medal.

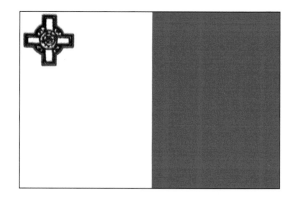

| MALTA | |
|---|---|
| Official Name: | Republic of Malta |
| Capital: | Valletta |
| Languages: | Maltese, English |
| Religions: | Roman Catholic |
| Exports: | Clothing, textiles, petroleum products |
| Imports: | Manufactured goods, machinery, food, petroleum |
| Highest Point: | 829 ft. (253 m) |
| Lowest Point: | Sea level |
| Area: | 122 sq. mi. (316 sq km) |

*The distinctive Maltese cross and the white cross on red of the Knights of Malta are both important symbols of Malta, an island in the Mediterranean.*

# AUSTRIA

Austria, once ruled by Charlemagne, was, for hundreds of years, a vast European empire until its dissolution in 1918. A popular legend says the flag's design was inspired by the bloodstained tunic of Duke Leopold V, and that the only part of the tunic to remain white was the area tucked under Leopold V's broad belt. Nevertheless, this national flag is one of the world's oldest banners; its colors have been used in the same form since at least A.D. 1230.

When the flag is raised by private citizens it appears unadorned; however, when used at official functions, it usually bears the Austrian coat of arms at its center.

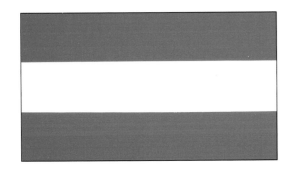

| AUSTRIA | |
|---|---|
| Official Name: | Republic of Austria |
| Capital: | Vienna |
| Languages: | German |
| Religions: | Roman Catholic, Protestant, Rhaeto-Romanu |
| Exports: | Iron and steel products, machinery, wood |
| Imports: | Machinery, chemicals, textiles, clothing |
| Highest Point: | 12,457 ft. (3,797 m) |
| Lowest Point: | 377 ft. (115 m) |
| Area: | 32,377 sq. mi. (83,824 sq km) |

# SWITZERLAND

Switzerland is divided into twenty-three cantons (districts), or more accurately, twenty full cantons and six half cantons. Three of these Swiss Confederation cantons formed a defensive league against Austrian rule in 1291. The flag was used by the Confederation as its battle flag in 1339 and by 1480, it became the dominant banner.

In 1648, the Confederation obtained its independence from the Holy Roman Empire. In 1848, the cantons adopted a federal constitution, which reserved a great deal of local control for each canton, and adopted the same square flag as the military flag of Switzerland. This flag remained the same over the years. Switzerland also has maintained an armed neutrality since 1815 and has not been involved in a foreign war since 1515.

Switzerland has strong heraldic traditions and every canton has its own arms and flag. Many of these regional flags contain emblems that have the same heraldic design as their arms. Bern's flag displays the image of a bear, and the flag flies all over the city. The head of a wild black ox with a red ring through its nose is displayed on Uri's flag. Lucerne uses the colors of white and blue on its flag and arms, although the colors are arranged horizontally on the flag and vertically on the arms.

| SWITZERLAND | |
|---|---|
| Official Name: | Swiss Confederation |
| Capital: | Bern |
| Languages: | German, French, Italian |
| Religions: | Roman Catholic, Protestant |
| Exports: | Machinery, electrical appliances, chemicals |
| Imports: | Machinery, metal and metal products, iron, food |
| Highest Point: | 15,203 ft. (4,634 m) |
| Lowest Point: | 633 ft. (193 m) |
| Area: | 15,943 sq. mi. (41,276 sq km) |

The Swiss flag is square when used on land, oblong when displayed on ships.

© Pam Hasegawa

# FRANCE

France's flag is the origin of a great many of the world's most renowned flags. France's traditional colors have always been blue, white, and red, despite the fact that all three weren't combined until the revolution of 1789.

The color blue is associated with St. Martin, and his white cross with a blue field was the prerevolutionary merchant flag. The color red is historically linked to St. Denis, and his red flag decorated with gold became known as the *oriflamme* (golden flames). The color white is associated with Joan of Arc, whose white standard led the French into battle in the Hundred Years' War against England and Burgundy. The traditional emblem of France was three fleurs-de-lis (lilies). Lilies were first used on French arms during the 1100s. During the Middle Ages, the French arms and banner were blue with many gold fleurs-de-lis about the field; however, after 1385, the shield carried only three fleurs-de-lis.

During and after the 1400s, French flags were adorned with crosses, the devices used by France during the Crusades. Civil flags of the 1600s and the 1700s bore a white cross on a blue field with the royal arms at the center of the flag. Military flags, such as the Bastille flag, also used the white cross. The national color was white because white was the color of the Bourbon dynasty, which ruled France from 1589 until the revolution. The royal standard was white and covered with gold fleurs-de-lis; the royal arms were placed at its center.

On July 14, 1789, Parisians stormed the Bastille wearing cockades of red and blue, the heraldic colors of the city of Paris. Three days later, it is said, the king placed a red and blue cockade next to the white Bourbon cockade on his hat; consequently, it was soon proposed that the national cockade be changed to red, blue, and white. The following year, French naval ships and popular flags began to display the colors. The French naval ensign was, of course, formerly white, so vertical stripes of red,

white, and blue were added to the canton. In 1794, the white field was dropped and the present order of the Tricolor stripes was adopted.

The Tricolor, whose stripes represent liberty, equality, and fraternity, continued to be used until 1814, when the monarchy was temporarily restored. However, Napoleon used the Tricolor until his final exile in 1815. In 1830, the Tricolor was restored and has remained in use since that time to inspire countless other flags of the world.

|  | FRANCE |
| --- | --- |
| Official Name: | French Republic |
| Capital: | Paris |
| Languages: | French |
| Religions: | Roman Catholic |
| Exports: | Machinery, transportation equipment, food |
| Imports: | Petroleum, machinery, chemicals |
| Highest Point: | 15,771 ft. (4,807 m) |
| Lowest Point: | -10 ft. (-3 m) |
| Area: | 211,208 sq. mi. (546,818 sq km) |

**KINGDOM OF FRANCE; STATE FLAG C. 1643–1790**

*Today it is difficult to believe that the Eiffel Tower was strongly criticized by many when it was built a century ago.*

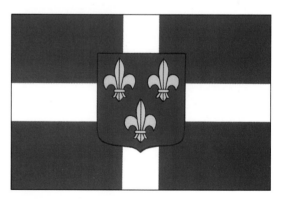

**KINGDOM OF FRANCE; CIVIL ENSIGN 1661–1790**

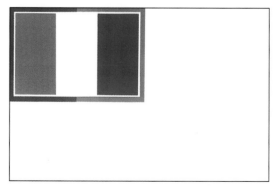

**FRANCE; WAR ENSIGN 1790–1794**

*ABOVE: The symbolic figure of Liberty leads the French to victory under the Tricolor in this famous ninteenth-century painting by Delacroix. (Detail)*

*BELOW: The Arch of Triumph in Paris commemorates the military victories of Napoleon; beneath is the tomb of France's Unknown Soldier.*

*ABOVE: This Monet painting shows the Rue St. Denis on June 30, 1878.*

*RIGHT: The Mediterranean town of Menton along the Côte d'Azur.*

*BELOW: The town of Dinan in Brittany, a region of France with a distinctive culture of its own.*

*BELOW: Villandry is one of many castles in the Loire valley in France.*

*LEFT: Grapes from Gironde, one of France's many wine-producing regions, near Bordeaux.*

*ABOVE: It took over a century to construct the cathedral at Amiens.*

## SPAIN

Spain's national flag colors are the dominant heraldic colors found on the arms of the kingdoms of Castile and Aragon, which were united in 1479 under Ferdinand II and Isabella I. This union led to the breaking of Moorish power, and by 1492 Spain was a bulwark of Roman Catholicism.

In 1785, a flag was created from these colors, and originally bore the arms of Castile and Léon in the yellow center stripe; the arms were deleted during the republic of 1931. During Francisco Franco's reign (1939–1975), Franco created new arms, which he placed on the state flag.

In 1975, the monarchy was restored, when Juan Carlos I ascended to the throne. In 1977, the arms were again modified, but were eventually replaced by the present ones in 1981. No arms appear on the flag when it is used for civil functions.

The Basque provinces, a region in northern Spain, are self-ruled. The people of the Basque provinces fly a flag that is a separatists' flag, known as the Ikurrina. This flag, inspired by the British Union Flag, has a red field that is divided by white and green crosses.

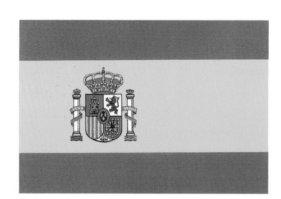

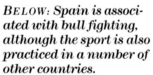

| SPAIN | |
|---|---|
| Official Name: | Kingdom of Spain |
| Capital: | Madrid |
| Languages: | Spanish |
| Religions: | Roman Catholic |
| Exports: | Iron and steel products, machinery, food |
| Imports: | Fuels, machinery, chemicals, iron, steel |
| Highest Point: | 12,188 ft. (3,715 m) |
| Lowest Point: | Sea level |
| Area: | 194,882 sq. mi. (504,549 sq km) |

*BELOW: Spain is associated with bull fighting, although the sport is also practiced in a number of other countries.*

*Karen McCunnall/Leo de Wys, Inc.*

# PORTUGAL

Portugal has been an independent state since the twelfth century. In 1830, Portugal adopted a vertical blue-and-white flag. Blue and white are the traditional colors of the country and are derived from the oldest and most central part of its arms. Portugal was a kingdom until 1910, when a revolution deposed King Manoel II. A republic was proclaimed at this time, and the flag's colors were changed to green and red. The green is said to date from the time of Prince Henry the Navigator (1394–1460), while the color red is a reminder of the revolution.

The original arms of Portugal consisted of a white shield bearing five blue shields, each with five white disks. This is associated with King Afonso Henriques who established Portugal as an independent power in the twelfth century. The red border with the yellow castles was added later by King Afonso III as an indication of his Spanish heritage.

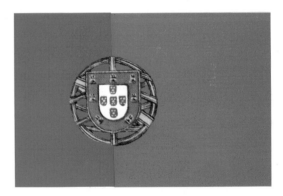

*OPPOSITE, TOP: The Catalan architect Gaudi did not live to see the completion of his Sagrada Familia Cathedral in Barcelona.*

*OPPOSITE, BOTTOM: The Moslem era in Spain produced few architectural treasures greater than the Court of Lions in the Alhambra Palace.*

*ABOVE: The Plaza of Spain in Seville.*

*RIGHT: The Palace and Tower in Seville.*

*Michael J. Howell/Envision*

| PORTUGAL | |
|---|---|
| Official Name: | Republic of Portugal |
| Capital: | Lisbon |
| Languages: | Portuguese |
| Religions: | Roman Catholic |
| Exports: | Clothing, cork, wood, food, wine |
| Imports: | Petroleum, machinery |
| Highest Point: | 7,713 ft. (2,351 m) |
| Lowest Point: | Sea level |
| Area: | 35,516 sq. mi. (91,951 sq km) |

# CHAPTER SIX

# *North America*

## *CANADA*

Jacques Cartier, the French explorer who discovered the Gulf of St. Lawrence in 1534, is considered to be the founder of Canada, even though English seaman John Cabot sighted Newfoundland in 1497 and the Vikings are credited with reaching the Atlantic Coast centuries before either explorer.

The French pioneered settlement of Canada with the establishment of Quebec City in 1608 and Montreal in 1642. In 1663, they declared New France a colony. Meanwhile, England, as part of its continued expansion, in 1717 acquired Acadia, later called Nova Scotia. Because of an extension of a European conflict between the two countries, England and France continued to fight on North American soil. The English defeated the French in 1759, took over Quebec, and finally gained control of the remainder of New France in 1763. Through the Quebec Act of 1774, the French retained the rights to their own language, religion, and civil law. In 1791, New France was divided into Upper and Lower Canada, which are now known as Ontario and Quebec respectively.

During the American Revolution, British presence increased in Canada as many Loyalists left the colonies and resettled there. While Upper and Lower Canada were attempting to settle problems of self-rule in the legislature, the War of 1812 intervened.

This war, a conflict between England and the United States, was fought mainly in Upper Canada and ended in a stalemate two years later.

Political agitation in 1837 culminated in rebellions in Upper and Lower Canada, and in 1837 the two territories were united into one colony, Canada. In 1867, the British North America (BNA) Act launched the Dominion of Canada, which consisted of Ontario, Quebec, and the former colonies of New Brunswick and Nova Scotia.

The Canadian colonies had held the right to internal self-rule since 1840, and adopted the BNA Act as the country's written constitution, establishing a system of government modeled after the British Parliament and a cabinet structure under control of the British. This status was referred to as "dominion status" within the British Commonwealth. On December 12, 1931, Canada gained full independence. At that time Canada did not take steps to create a distinctive national flag as some of the other dominions had done.

Until February 15, 1965, Canada's unofficial national flag consisted of the British Red Ensign with the Dominion's shield of arms in the fly. The upper section of the shield was similar to the British Royal Standard, except that its fourth quarter bore three fleurs-de-lis, gold on blue, representing France. Below this, three maple leaves appeared on a white field.

In May 1964, Prime Minister Lester Pearson proposed adopting a new flag, one that would symbolize a nonaligned, wholly independent Canada. Canadians responded with 4,200 suggestions, and for the remainder of 1964, a public debate raged until a majority vote was reached in Parliament. The design of Canada's first true national flag, hoisted on February 15, 1965, was chosen for two reasons. The first reason was that the maple leaf had been a symbol of Canada since the early 1800s and the second was that red and white had been the official colors of Canada since 1921.

Canada's ten provinces and the territories each have their own flag. These flags often utilize emblems belonging to the mother country combined with regional symbols. The province and territory flags appear in the order in which they were formed.

*This totem pole is in Vancouver, but the entire province of British Columbia has hundreds of similar carvings by Native Americans.*

| **CANADA** | |
|---|---|
| Official Name: | Canada |
| Capital: | Ottawa |
| Languages: | English, French |
| Religions: | Roman Catholic, United Church, Anglican |
| Exports: | Transportation equipment, wood, paper, food, gas |
| Imports: | Transportation equipment, machinery, petroleum equipment |
| Highest Point: | 19,524 ft. (5,951 m) |
| Lowest Point: | Sea level |
| Area: | 3,831,033 sq. mi. (9,918,544 sq km) |

*LEFT: The Maple Leaf Flag flies proudly on Canada Day, the first of July.*

*BELOW: Calgary is one of many cities in Canada's Prairie provinces that have witnessed extensive growth in the past few decades.*

# Canadian Provinces

## Quebec

Quebec's flag symbolism is directly derived from prerevolutionary France, whose civil ensign used a blue field with a white cross and an emblem of the fleur-de-lis. The flag, evolved from earlier models, was officially adopted on January 21, 1948.

## Nova Scotia

Nova Scotia received its own coat of arms in 1625 from Charles I, but this was overlooked at the time of federation. The coat of arms was reintroduced in 1929 and, since then, a banner of the province's arms (which combines two Scottish emblems, the rampant lion, and St. Andrew's saltire) has been used as a flag.

## New Brunswick

New Brunswick received its arms in 1868. The banner, based on those arms, which depicts heraldic symbols of a ship (called a lymphad) and a rampant lion, is used as a provincial flag, which was adopted on February 24, 1965. The arms were revised in 1984.

## Ontario

The maple leaf was first used as a Canadian symbol in Ontario, but the province did not have a flag of its own until 1965. At that time it selected the British Red Ensign and added the provincial shield in the center of the fly. The shield is green with three yellow maple leaves below a white band bearing the red cross of St. George.

## Manitoba

Until 1870, Manitoba was called the Red River Settlement. Its arms were adopted in 1905. On May 12, 1966, Manitoba's provincial flag bearing its arms on the British Red Ensign was made official.

## British Columbia

In 1866, British Columbia and Vancouver Island became a colony. In 1871, the colony joined the federation. British Columbia's arms date back to 1906, and a banner of the arms has been used as a provincial flag since 1960.

## Prince Edward Island

Prince Edward Island was part of Nova Scotia until 1769 and did not join the federation until 1873. On May 30, 1905, its arms, depicting an oak tree and three saplings, were granted. On March 24, 1964, its banner of arms, reflecting its geographical location, was adopted as the provincial flag.

## Alberta

Alberta was originally part of Rupert's Land and, later, a part of the North-West Territories. In 1905, the District of Alberta joined with Athabasca to create a new province. In 1907, the province's arms, depicting the prairie of Alberta, were granted. On June 1, 1968, the provincial flag was adopted.

## Saskatchewan

Saskatchewan, once part of the North-West Territories, became a province in 1905 and obtained its arms one year later. Its flag, the result of a design competition, depicts the shield of arms (three wheat sheaves) and the prairie lily, the provincial plant badge.

## Newfoundland and Labrador

Newfoundland and Labrador was a separate dominion from 1931 to 1934, when the territory reverted to British rule. Newfoundland and Labrador became a Canadian province in 1949. Its flag was designed in 1980 by a local artist and has no connection to its arms.

## Northwest Territories

The Northwest Territories were once part of the Hudson's Bay Territory and in 1880, along with the Arctic islands, were annexed to Canada. In 1956, the Northwest Territories received its arms. On January 31, 1969, the shield from the arms was centered on a flag chosen in a competition. The shield carries emblems representing the North-West Passage through the ice, the timberline between frozen ice and forest, mining, and fur trapping. The flag, except for the difference in color and center symbol, has the same construction as the national flag of Canada.

## Yukon

In 1898, the Yukon became a separate territory after the renowned gold rush. In 1956, it obtained a coat of arms. Later, a competition was held to select a flag design, but the winning flag, bearing the entire coat of arms, wasn't adopted until March 1, 1968. The green represents the Yukon's forests; white, its snow; and blue, its lakes.

**PROVINCIAL FLAG OF QUEBEC**

**PROVINCIAL FLAG OF NOVA SCOTIA**

**PROVINCIAL FLAG OF PRINCE EDWARD ISLAND**

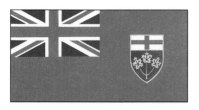

PROVINCIAL flag of ONTARIO

TERRITORIAL FLAG OF THE NORTHWEST TERRITORIES

PROVINCIAL flag of MANITOBA

TERRITORIAL FLAG OF YUKON TERRITORY

PROVINCIAL flag of BRITISH COLUMBIA

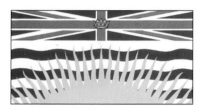

PROVINCIAL flag of NEW BRUNSWICK

PROVINCIAL flag of ALBERTA

PROVINCIAL FLAG OF SASKATCHEWAN

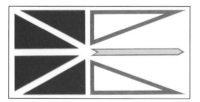

PROVINCIAL FLAG OF NEWFOUNDLAND AND LABRADOR

The lighthouse at Peggy's Cove, Nova Scotia.

# UNITED STATES OF AMERICA

The Stars and Stripes flag of the United States of America was created in 1777, although several earlier versions of this flag were used by the colonies as they struggled for independence from British rule. Since its inception, the Stars and Stripes flag has had a major impact on flag design worldwide. It was one of the first flags to use the colors red, white, and blue to symbolize a liberal, democratic, secular republic—as well as being the first national flag to use the five-pointed star as an emblem. The flag was also the first to use a star and stripe to represent a member state.

The history of the United States' national flag, called by many the Stars and Stripes, is so clouded by myth that the true facts are obscured and, therefore, are impossible to establish. Consequently, we may never know the answers to the following questions: Who designed the Stars and Stripes? What is the significance of the flag's colors? Who actually made the first flag, and was it ever hoisted for land battle during the American Revolution?

One thing is clear. The Stars and Stripes flag was created as a result of a resolution adopted on June 14, 1777. The resolution stated: "Resolved: that the Flag of the united states be 13 stripes alternate red and white, that the Union be 13 stars white in a blue field representing a new constellation."

At this point, Congress did not say what the colors meant, who would design the flag, nor did it give instructions as to the positioning of the stars. There was also no information about the appropriate uses of the flag. In fact, the resolution establishing the flag wasn't published until months later, on September 2, 1777. Use of the flag grew slowly. It was not regularly carried by the army and few public buildings displayed any flag. Ships and fortresses were generally the only places one could see the Stars and Stripes during the first decade of its existence.

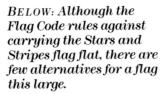

| UNITED STATES OF AMERICA | |
|---|---|
| Official Name: | The United States of America |
| Capital: | Washington, D.C. |
| Languages: | English |
| Religions: | Protestant, Roman Catholic, Jewish, others |
| Exports: | Machinery, chemicals, transportation equipment |
| Imports: | Petroleum, machinery, transportation equipment |
| Highest Point: | 20,320 ft. (6,194 m) |
| Lowest Point: | -282 ft. (-86 m) |
| Area: | 3,679,245 sq. mi. (9,525,565 sq km) |

*BELOW: Although the Flag Code rules against carrying the Stars and Stripes flag flat, there are few alternatives for a flag this large.*

*ABOVE: Technological achievement and the love of Old Glory are reflected in this photograph taken on the Moon.*

*LEFT: A ring of fifty United States flags surrounds the Washington Monument in the nation's capital.*

© Christopher C. Bain

*BELOW: Each of the five armed forces of the United States has a distinctive flag of its own.*

© Christopher C. Bain

*LEFT: The largest United States flag (200' × 400' [60 × 120 m]) has never been hoisted, but must be displayed on the ground.*

© Arthur Hill/Visuals Unlimited

# The Story of the Stars and Stripes

The first flag of the United States was the Continental Colors, sometimes incorrectly referred to as the Grand Union or the Cambridge Flag. Despite its use from late 1775 until mid-1777, it was never officially sanctioned by the Continental Congress. This flag was an alteration of the British Meteor Flag, and bore in its blue canton the red cross of St. George and the white cross of St. Andrew, which combined to form the British Union Flag (see **United Kingdom**). The field had thirteen alternating red and white horizontal stripes. This flag was first raised on Prospect Hill, in Somerville, Massachusetts, on January 1, 1776, when the Continental Army came into formal existence.

One flag that has caused a storm of controversy has been housed for 150 years at a public library in Easton, Pennsylvania. This flag has all the elements of the national flag, but in reversed order, that is, thirteen red and white stripes in the canton and thirteen white stars centered in a blue field.

The revolutionary Sons of Liberty organized in 1765 to oppose the Stamp Tax. A flag of four white and five red stripes used by them recalled No. 45 of the *North Briton* in which civil liberties had been outspokenly endorsed. Later flags had thirteen stripes for the number of American colonies. A rattlesnake with thirteen rattles on its tail was sometimes used as an American symbol. In 1775, at Concord, Massachusetts, minutemen from Bedford, Massachusetts, are reported to have unfurled a crimson flag upon which was a silver arm brandishing a sword whose blade was silver with a golden hilt. This flag also depicted silver balls and clouds and a gold ribbon. In Charlestown, Massachusetts, the Sons of Liberty hoisted a plain red flag with a green pine tree in its canton. The pine tree symbol was used by New England as early as 1686. It represented an important part of local commerce and appeared on the famous New England pine

tree shilling. Some even proposed the pine tree flag for the united American colonies.

Another early United States flag had a yellow field with green grass in which sat a brown rattlesnake with a red tongue. Underneath the snake was the warning, in black lettering, "Don't Tread on Me." Although first used by Commodore Esek Hopkins, the first commander in chief of the navy, this flag is often called the Gadsden Flag because Colonel Christopher Gadsden had a copy of it made for the South Carolina Provincial Congress in February 1776.

For many years it was believed that the "Bennington Flag" had been carried at the battle near that Vermont town on August 16, 1777. It had seven white and six red horizontal stripes with a blue canton of unusual design. In addition to thirteen white stars it incorporated the figure 76. Recent examination of the flag suggests that it probably was made in 1826 on the fiftieth anniversary of the Declaration of Independence.

This flag was used until 1795, when the states of Vermont and Kentucky were admitted into the Union. At this time, President Washington signed into law an act of Congress that stated after May 1, 1795, the flag should have fifteen stripes, alternating red and white, and fifteen white stars on a blue field. Soon, other new states were admitted, and it quickly became clear that the flag would become too crowded with stripes. Congress then decreed that after July 4, 1818, the flag should have thirteen stripes to symbolize the original thirteen states and twenty stars to symbolize the Union's twenty states, but that whenever a new state was admitted into the union, a new star should be added on the Fourth of July following the state's admission. No star is identified with a specific state, and there is no law designating the permanent arrangement of the stars. However, since 1912, whenever a new state has been added, the new design has been announced by presidential order.

*UNITED STATES; NATIONAL FLAG 1776-1777*

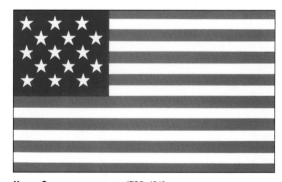

*UNITED STATES; NATIONAL FLAG 1777-1795*

*UNITED STATES; NATIONAL FLAG 1795-1818*

*UNITED STATES; NATIONAL FLAG 1859-1861*

*LEFT: H. C. Chandler,* The Signing of the Constitution.

*BOTTOM, LEFT: For African-American soldiers, the Civil War was a struggle for liberty as well as preservation of the Union.*

*BOTTOM, RIGHT: Millions of new Americans saw Old Glory displayed in the main hall at Ellis Island.*

# Legends About the United States Flag

## Who Designed the Flag?

It is not known with absolute certainty who designed the United States flag, that is, who substituted for the Union Jack a blue canton with thirteen white stars. Nevertheless, Francis Hopkinson has a strong claim to be that designer. He submitted a bill to Congress for having designed a number of symbols, including the national flag. His claim was not accepted, but the rejection was not based on congressional-denial of his having created the design. Hopkinson was a signer of the Declaration of Independence, a member of the Naval Board, a congressman, poet and essayist, and lawyer. Although many Americans believe that Betsy Ross designed the flag, that claim was never made by her family.

## Who Called the Flag "Old Glory"?

A sea captain from Salem, Massachusetts, William Driver, is said to have in 1824 raised the flag on his brig, the *Charles Dog-gett,* and pronounced, "I name thee Old Glory." Another version of this story is that Captain Driver named the flag "Old Glory" when it was presented to him by his mother on his twenty-first birthday on March 17, 1824.

## Who Really Sewed the First United States Flag?

A widely publicized legend says that Betsy Ross, a Philadelphia seamstress, received a call prior to the signing of the Declaration of Independence from a committee of the Congress, who requested that she make the first Stars and Stripes. This story was first made public by a grandson of Mrs. Ross in 1870, but historians have not been able to locate any record of the request or a receipt

*Despite historians' disbelief, Betsy Ross is firmly entrenched in American legend as having sewn the first American flag for George Washington.*

for payment. Despite the lack of concrete evidence, this story is firmly implanted in American folklore.

Another well-documented story about a flag maker concerns Mary Young Pickersgill, the daughter of Rebecca Flower Young. In 1807, Mary and her mother, both widows, moved to Baltimore, Maryland. Once there, Mary quickly advertised as a "flag, banner, and pennant maker" and began making flags for local shipowners. In 1813, Mary Pickersgill made the Star-Spangled Banner, the flag that flew over Fort McHenry during the War of 1812 (this was the flag that United States national anthem author Francis Scott Key saw in the "dawn's early light"). This garrison flag was thirty feet (9 m) in hoist (height) by forty-two feet (12.6 m) fly (the length from staff to the outer edge of the flag). The flag

had fifteen five-pointed stars, each two feet (60 cm) from point to point, and was arranged in five indented parallel lines, three stars in each line. The flag had fifteen instead of thirteen stripes; each stripe was nearly two feet (60 cm) in width.

Because Mary Pickersgill's original receipt was found, there is no doubt that she did indeed make the Star-Spangled Banner for the sum of $405.90. This price includes the payment for a second flag, believed to be a storm flag. The Star-Spangled Banner is presently on display at the Smithsonian Institution in Washington, D.C.

# The Star-Spangled Banner: A National Anthem

On the evening of September 13, 1814, Francis Scott Key, a lawyer from Georgetown, District of Columbia, was detained aboard an American truce vessel on the Chesapeake Bay, near the flagship of a British admiral who was in the process of attempting to capture Baltimore, Maryland. The first item on the agenda was, however, the attack on Fort McHenry, a military installation guarding the city's sea approach. Because the need for secrecy was great, Key was prohibited from returning to shore.

The British bombarded the fort throughout the stormy night, and Key, from his vantage point, witnessed an immense British fleet shell a small American fort that had few long-range cannons to protect itself. The cause seemed lost. However, as morning came, Key saw the American flag, made by Mary Pickersgill, flying over the fort, proof that the American commander, Major George Armistead, and his troops had withstood the attack. Inspired by this sight, Key penned a few lines about the siege and the sight. The *Baltimore Patriot and Evening Advertiser* published the finished poem the following week under the title "The Defense of Fort McHenry."

*The Pledge of Allegiance was developed for Columbus Day in 1892, the 400th anniversary of the explorer's arrival in the New World.*

Soon, set to the tune of a well-known British song, "To Anacreon in Heaven," Key's poem became a popular United States patriotic song. An act of Congress in 1931 declared "The Star-Spangled Banner" to be the national anthem of the United States. While there is a popular movement afoot to change the anthem to "America the Beautiful," the "Star-Spangled Banner" remains an important reminder of the United States' national heritage.

## The Pledge of Allegiance

*I pledge allegiance to the flag of the United States of America and to the republic for which it stands, one nation under God, indivisible, with liberty and justice for all.*

This is the official version of the Pledge of Allegiance, which developed from the original pledge that was first published in 1892 in an issue of the *Youth's Companion*, a weekly Boston-based magazine. The original pledge contained the phrase "my flag," which was altered more than thirty years later to read "the flag of the United States of America." In 1954, an act of Congress added the words "under God."

Like much of the information about the United States flag, there is controversy about the authorship of this pledge. In 1917, the *Youth's Companion* reported that the original draft of the pledge was penned by one James B. Upham, who died in 1910. In 1923, Francis Bellamy, a former member of the *Youth's Companion* editorial staff, claimed to have written the pledge himself; in 1957, the Library of Congress issued a report naming Bellamy as the author.

## Prohibited Uses of the Flag

In the United States, there are strict regulations about the use of the flag. Despite the fact that the Stars and Stripes originated in 1777, it wasn't until 150 years had passed that there was a serious effort to codify its usage. In 1923, the War Department issued a circular on the rules of flag usage, and these rules were adopted in their entirety on June 14, 1923, by a conference of patriotic organizations in Washington, D.C. On June 22, 1942, a joint resolution of Congress, amended by Public Law 94-344 July 7, 1976, codified "existing rules and customs pertaining to the display and use of the flag...."

Throughout the years there has been much controversy about flag ownership and proper display. During the tumultuous 1960s, protesters not only wore the Stars and Stripes but also burned the flag as a symbol of their dissatisfaction with United States involvement in Vietnam. Songs, such as "The Fightin' Side of Me" written and sung by Merle Haggard, have been written in defense of hard-liners about this issue, which, to this day, is still unsolved. Many people in the United States believe the flag to be an object of near-worship, and that any use that is not one of pure reverence is punishable. Many citizens believe that a flag is a mere symbol and that as a citizen, one is entitled to express oneself. These people believe the flag to be an extension of self-expression and that a country that has fought to gain individual freedom should not dictate when it concerns the symbol of that freedom, the Stars and Stripes. Needless to say, in the United States, the flag is a subject that is gingerly approached, even by the Supreme Court, which ruled in 1990 that the Constitution did protect those who would burn the flag as a form of self-expression.

*LEFT: Mount Rushmore in South Dakota has the sculpted heads of Presidents Washington, Jefferson, Theodore Roosevelt and Lincoln.*

*BELOW: The Statue of Liberty is an American symbol as well loved as the Stars and Stripes.*

*LEFT: The lighthouse at Pemaquid Point in Maine.*

*RIGHT: Another famous landmark: the Golden Gate Bridge in San Francisco.*

*BELOW, RIGHT: Thomas Jefferson was proud of his design for the buildings at the University of Virginia in Charlottesville.*

*BELOW: One of the United States' most famous natural wonders: the Grand Canyon.*

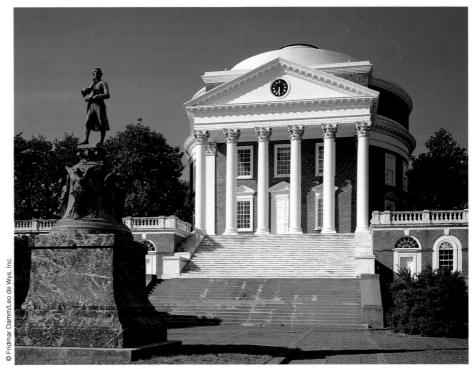

# Making Clothes into Flags

During war, prisoners often give special attention to the flag for which they have fought. During the American Revolution, an American prisoner created a small, handmade flag with thirteen roughly made embroidered stars and a white appliquéd ribbon that served as stripes against a blue and red background.

In the Virginia campaign of 1863, the men of the Sixteenth Connecticut Regiment, while being detained for capture, tore up their beloved flag and distributed small pieces of it among themselves, rather than permit their colors to fall into enemy hands. After the war ended and they were released, these men reassembled and restored the flag to its original form.

In 1973, Air Force Lieutenant Colonel John Dramisi of Philadelphia, Pennsylva-

*In no other country does the flag permeate everyday life as much as in the United States.*

*Traditionally, the figure of Uncle Sam is dressed in the colors and design of the national flag.*

nia, exhibited a small American flag he had constructed while a prisoner of war (POW) in Hanoi during the Vietnam War. Dramisi had used blue material from his jacket and red from a pair of women's undergarments. Using copper wire and a needle, he sewed on fifty white stars made from an unraveled towel. It was this flag that he and his fellow POWs saluted each and every evening until they were free.

Many types of flags were hoisted over the young territories and the high seas before 1777, the year the First Continental Congress met and codified into law the color and design of the United States flag. However, because the circular placement of the stars was not mentioned in the resolution, many strange and colorful flags appeared over the next seventy years throughout the struggling colonies.

A great variety of fabrics were used for early flags. Silk had to be imported and wool bunting for flags was not manufactured in the United States until after the Civil War. Until the 1840s all flags were sewn by hand and many were rather crudely made, especially on board ship where replacements were needed during long voyages. Nevertheless, Americans began to make and use their national flag because it symbolized the people rather than simply the government. This meant that very early in American history flags came into popular use, while in many other parts of the world this was not true until the second half of the twentieth century.

In those early days, both men and women sewed flags. While some were made in haste and were quite primitive, others were constructed by craftspeople

*Antique shops are a good source for flag-related collectibles.*

and were beautiful and well made. The Bennington Flag was one such example. This flag was produced from linen made from Vermont flax; this construction material made the flag a true product of the infant country. It wasn't until 1837 that bunting (a lightweight, loosely woven fabric) was produced in the United States, but by 1900, more than 120,000 yards (108,000 m) of this material had been sewn into the nation's flags. After the end of World War II, bunting was replaced by nylon as the main flag-making material.

In 1780, Colonel William Washington informed his fiancée, Miss Jane Elliott, that he had no flag with which to lead his troops into battle. Miss Elliott promptly cut a square of red damask fabric from a chair and fringed the edges. She then tacked it onto a pole and presented it to Colonel Washington, who then carried this flag into the Battle of Cowpens at Eutaw Springs, Virginia.

Eight years later, on August 29, 1778, it was reported that Captain Abraham Swarthout sent a note to Colonel Peter Gansevoort in which the captain requested about eight yards (7 m) of broadcloth from the local commissary. This broadcloth was to be used to replace the captain's blue cloak, which was used as the colors of Fort Schuyler in New York. This blue cloak had served as the fort's colors for a year, when the fort had been called Fort Stanwix, and had probably been a Grand Union flag in design. The blue had come from the captain's coat, the white from the soldiers' shirts, and the red from a flannel petticoat belonging to Mrs. Gansevoort.

Today, flags are mass-produced and, because they are inexpensive, are readily available. However, there is also a revived interest in the craft of flag making and many people today do indeed sew their own flags, not only to create an art object, but perhaps, to experience the same feelings of pride that these colonists had when they hoisted a flag of their own making.

*A mailbox with an American flag motif, Homestead, Florida.*

*The flag appears as a theme in folk art, advertising, and decoration.*

*This flag was made by children and attached to a fence at their school.*

# Dependencies of the United States

## American Samoa

American Samoa, ruled by the United States since 1900, is made up of six Polynesian islands located in the Pacific Ocean. An unincorporated territory, American Samoa is located farthest south of all land that falls under United States sovereignty. When the islands obtained internal self-government, the flag was adopted. The emblem is a bald eagle clutching in its talons a fly whisk and a war club, which are symbols of authority in this territory. The other colors are the same as the Stars and Stripes.

## Palau

Palau, a republic since 1981, is a group of islands located in the Pacific Ocean. The flag, the result of a design competition, was adopted in 1980 and depicts a golden full moon on a blue field, which represents national unity and the end of foreign domination.

## Guam

Guam is a Pacific Ocean island that was seized from Spain in 1898. The wife of a naval officer designed the flag, which was adopted in 1917. The flag depicts part of the territorial seal, a beach scene with a view often incorrectly thought to include a hill called "Lover's Leap."

## North Marianas

The North Marianas is a group of islands located to the east of the Philippines in the Pacific Ocean. These islands were, until 1976, a district of the United States Territory of the Pacific Islands. They are now a commonwealth state in association with the United States. The flag was adopted in 1972 and altered in 1989. The blue background is for the Pacific Ocean. The white star standing for the commonwealth is set against a latte stone, symbolic of the ancient Chamorro culture in the islands. The wreath of flowers was added to symbolize the Carolinian people who also live there.

## United States Virgin Islands

The U.S. Virgin Islands are located between the Atlantic Ocean and the Caribbean Sea and are an unincorporated territory of the United States. The flag, adopted in 1921, was designed by a sailor who worked for the governor. The design is a simpler version of the Great Seal of the United States of America, and bears the initials 'VI' for, of course, the Virgin Islands.

*St. Thomas is part of the Virgin Islands. It was purchased by the United States in 1917 from Denmark.*

## Puerto Rico

Puerto Rico, located in the Caribbean Sea, was captured from Spain in 1898. In 1952, Puerto Rico became a commonwealth with full internal self-government. The flag, which uses the colors of the Stars and Stripes, was first used in 1895 by a Puerto Rican nationalist group seeking aid from the United States. The flag was adopted officially in 1952.

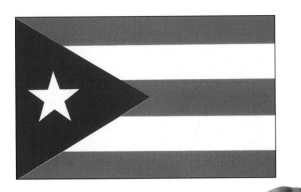

| PUERTO RICO | |
|---|---|
| Official Name: | Commonwealth of Puerto Rico |
| Capital: | San Juan |
| Languages: | Spanish, English |
| Religions: | Roman Catholic |
| Exports: | Clothing, textiles, electrical equipment, sugar |
| Imports: | Petroleum, food |
| Highest Point: | 4,390 ft. (1,338 m) |
| Lowest Point: | Sea level |
| Area: | 3,515 sq. mi. (9,100 sq km) |

## MEXICO

Mexico was once called New Spain, when Spanish rule (see **Central and South America**) extended even into North America. Before the Spanish conquistadors arrived in 1519, Mexico was the center of advanced Indian civilizations. The Mayans, moving up from the Yucatán, built gigantic stone pyramids and invented a working calendar. Another early culture, the Toltecs, was defeated by the Aztecs, who founded Tenochtitlan, what is now Mexico City, in A.D. 1325. The Aztecs were conquered by

Hernando Cortés, the Spanish conquistador, between 1519 and 1521.

After three hundred years of Spanish dominance, the Mexican people revolted under the leadership of Miguel Hidalgo y Costilla in 1810 and, later, under General Augustin Iturbide, who led them to independence in 1821, and then made himself Emperor Augustin I. In 1823, a republic was founded when Augustin I stepped down.

During the struggle for independence, Mexico used many different flags. Hidalgo had raised a religious banner with the Virgin of Guadalupe as his flag. Troops commanded by General Iturbide used a diagonal tricolor of white-green-red, among other flags. The first national flag, however, dating from 1815 to 1821, had a red border surrounding blue and white rectangles. Finally, in 1821 the vertical tricolor of green-white-red was adopted to symbolize

the "Three Guarantees"—independence, religion, and union. This flag bore the Mexican eagle with a crown on its head to indicate that the country was an empire. The crown was omitted after 1823, and different artistic renditions of the eagle were introduced over the years. Mexico again became an empire under Maximilian I in the 1860s, but his imperial flags were defeated by Mexican nationalists who opposed the European monarch. The present form of the emblem on the Mexican flag was adopted in 1968 at the time of the Olympic Games held in Mexico City.

The national flag and the president's standard display on the central band an eagle perched atop a prickly pear plant, grasping a snake in its beak. This device is a reference to an old Aztec legend that says the people should build their city where the eagle was seen doing this.

*A Mexican dancer in typical costume.*

| MEXICO | |
|---|---|
| Official Name: | United Mexican States |
| Capital: | Mexico City |
| Languages: | Spanish |
| Religions: | Roman Catholic, Protestant |
| Exports: | Petroleum, cotton, coffee, minerals |
| Imports: | Machinery, industrial vehicles, international goods |
| Highest Point: | 18,701 ft. (5,700 m) |
| Lowest Point: | -26 ft. (-8 m) |
| Area: | 761,604 sq. mi. (1,971,792 sq km) |

The palace at Chichen Itza, Mexico.

A Mayan statue from Oaxaca, Mexico.

The Temple of Warriors is a reminder of Mexico's Aztec past.

A church in Chachalachas, Vera Cruz, Mexico.

*The cloak of the Virgin of Guadalupe is venerated in this cathedral in Mexico.*

© Evan Agostini

 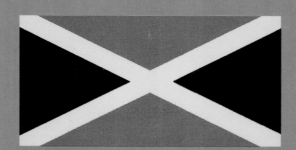 

 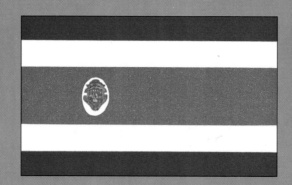 

# CHAPTER SEVEN

# *Central America*

The Mayan civilization thrived from the first millennium until the arrival of the Spanish in the area now called Central America. With the arrival of Christopher Columbus in 1502, this region became the Spanish provinces of the Captaincy-General of Guatemala. In 1821, the Captaincy-General of Guatemala became free from Spain, but immediately became a part of the new Mexican Empire.

By 1823, all of the former Spanish-held provinces (Costa Rica, El Salvador, Guatemala, Honduras, and Nicaragua) except Chiapas (which became a Mexican state) had freed themselves from Mexican rule and formed the United Provinces of Central America, a confederation based on Guatemala. This group adopted a common flag, a horizontal tribar of blue, white, and blue with the arms in the center. The two blue bands represent the Pacific Ocean and the Caribbean Sea.

This loose federation existed until 1839, when it separated into independent nations. Each country, however, still retains use of the tribar, but adds an emblem or alters the flag's style to convey its individuality.

# GUATEMALA

In what is now the capital of Guatemala, Guatemala City, the independence of Central America was proclaimed on September 15, 1821. After a brief period of Mexican rule, Guatemala and the other Central American provinces formed the United Provinces of Central America and hoisted a blue-and-white flag, a variant of which Guatemala used until 1851. At that time, red and yellow stripes were added to the flag and remained there until 1871. In 1871, the first colors were readopted, although they were arranged vertically to distinguish them from the other states' flags.

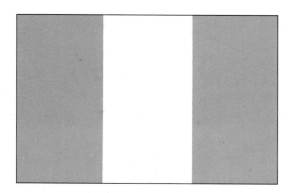

| GUATEMALA | |
|---|---|
| Official Name: | Republic of Guatemala |
| Capital: | Guatemala |
| Languages: | Spanish, indigenous |
| Religions: | Roman Catholic, Protestant, indigenous |
| Exports: | Coffee, cotton, sugar |
| Imports: | Manufactured goods, transportation equipment, fuels |
| Highest Point: | 13,845 ft. (4,220 m) |
| Lowest Point: | Sea level |
| Area: | 42,042 sq. mi. (108,847 sq km) |

# BELIZE

Belize (called British Honduras until 1973) was the last British colony to gain freedom in North America. Belize was granted its arms in 1907 while it was a colony. The arms have been modified in later years. Originally, on the flag adopted by the People's United party, which resembles the present flag without the two red stripes, the Union Flag was removed from the canton of the shield. In 1950, a wreath of fifty leaves was placed around the arms to symbolize the beginning of the struggle for independence from Britain. The beginning of the struggle for local self-government began in 1950 and later the wreath around the central emblem was given exactly fifty leaves to commemorate that date. When Belize eventually gained independence in 1981, the red stripes were added and some modifications were made in the coat of arms appearing in the center of the flag. These emblems were derived from the flag of the United Democratic party. In this way, the flag combines the colors of the two parties.

| BELIZE | |
|---|---|
| Official Name: | Belize |
| Capital: | Belmopan |
| Languages: | English, Spanish, indigenous |
| Religions: | Roman Catholic, Anglican, Protestant |
| Exports: | Sugar, clothing, fish, citrus fruits |
| Imports: | Food, machinery, consumer goods, transportation equipment |
| Highest Point: | 3,680 ft. (1,121 m) |
| Lowest Point: | Sea level |
| Area: | 8,866 sq. mi. (22,954 sq km) |

# EL SALVADOR

El Salvador became independent from Spain in 1821. From 1835 to 1865, El Salvador used the flag of the Federation. In 1865, this nation began using a flag that closely resembled the United States' Stars and Stripes, but in 1912, it readopted the Central American colors.

| EL SALVADOR | |
|---|---|
| Official Name: | Republic of El Salvador |
| Capital: | San Salvador |
| Languages: | Spanish |
| Religions: | Roman Catholic |
| Exports: | Coffee, cotton, sugar |
| Imports: | Machinery, petroleum, fertilizer, motor vehicles |
| Highest Point: | 7,933 ft. (2,418 m) |
| Lowest Point: | Sea level |
| Area: | 8,124 sq. mi. (21,033 sq km) |

# HONDURAS

Honduras became independent from Spain in 1821. Its national flag is the flag of the United Provinces of Central America. In 1866, the five stars (one for each Central American country) were added with the hope that the original Federation states would reunite in the future.

| HONDURAS | |
|---|---|
| Official Name: | Republic of Honduras |
| Capital: | Tegucigalpa |
| Languages: | Spanish |
| Religions: | Roman Catholic |
| Exports: | Bananas, coffee, wood, meat |
| Imports: | Manufactured goods, transportation equipment, chemicals |
| Highest Point: | 9,347 ft. (2,849 m) |
| Lowest Point: | Sea level |
| Area: | 43,277 sq. mi. (112,044 sq km) |

# NICARAGUA

Nicaragua became independent from Spain in 1821. The national flag, which came into use in 1838, is in the Central American configuration and, like the original flag of the United Provinces, its arms are in the center. The arms of Nicaragua are made up of a golden triangle with five volcanoes (representing the five states); a rainbow (peace); and a cap of Liberty. Around this triangle is the name of the state and the words "America Central" (Central America).

In 1854, a new flag of yellow-white-red stripes was adopted, soon to be replaced by a blue-white-blue flag with a large central red star. Eventually the original design was reestablished in 1858, with subsequent modifications in the design of the coat of arms. The latest change was made in 1971.

| NICARAGUA | |
|---|---|
| Official Name: | Republic of Nicaragua |
| Capital: | Managua |
| Languages: | Spanish, English |
| Religions: | Roman Catholic |
| Exports: | Cotton, coffee, sugar, meat |
| Imports: | Food, chemicals and pharmaceuticals, machinery |
| Highest Point: | 6,913 ft. (2,107 m) |
| Lowest Point: | Sea level |
| Area: | 50,193 sq. mi. (129,820 sq km) |

# COSTA RICA

Costa Rica became independent from Spain in 1821. For the next two decades five different flags were used. All were striped flags of white and blue except for the very first (1823–1824), which had a six-pointed red star in the center of a white field. In 1842, Costa Rica adopted the design of the defunct Federation but with its own emblems.

The flag (and arms) were redesigned in 1848; a red stripe was added, an influence of the French Revolution. The flag also bears, close to the hoist, a white oval enclosing the national arms, a shield on which are three volcanoes between the Pacific Ocean and the Caribbean Sea. On each body of water is a sailing vessel and, in the blue sky, are seven stars that represent the provinces.

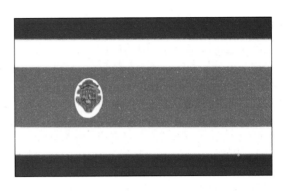

*The tropical rain forest at Carillo National Park in Costa Rica.*

| COSTA RICA | |
|---|---|
| Official Name: | Republic of Costa Rica |
| Capital: | San José |
| Languages: | Spanish |
| Religions: | Roman Catholic |
| Exports: | Coffee, bananas, beef, sugar |
| Imports: | Manufactured goods, machinery, transportation equipment |
| Highest Point: | 12,530 ft. (3,819 m) |
| Lowest Point: | Sea level |
| Area: | 19,730 sq. mi. (51,081 sq km) |

# PANAMA

Panama was a Spanish colony until it became a province of Colombia in 1821. In 1903, Panama declared its independence from Colombia and, with the support of the United States, became an independent republic in which the Panama Canal was to be built.

The original proposal for a Panamanian flag was based on the Stars and Stripes. It had red and yellow stripes with a blue canton showing two golden suns linked together—a symbol of the role Panama was to play in linking East and West. Nevertheless the first national flag, designed by Manuel Amador, was basically like the design now in use, which was adopted in 1904. The flag's colors are said to represent the Liberal and Conservative (or *Colorados* [reds]) parties of Panama. The white symbolizes peace; the blue star represents authority and legality. The flag has been flown in the Canal Zone since 1960 and has been the only flag flown there since 1979.

© John Hutchinson/Envision

*ABOVE: A ship passing through the locks of the Panama Canal.*

*BELOW: A mola, fabric folk art of the Cuna Indians of Panama.*

© Iraida Icaza/Leo de Wys, Inc.

|  | PANAMA |
|---|---|
| Official Name: | Republic of Panama |
| Capital: | Panama City |
| Languages: | Spanish, English |
| Religions: | Roman Catholic, Protestant |
| Exports: | Petroleum products, bananas, sugar |
| Imports: | Manufactured goods, petroleum, machinery, food |
| Highest Point: | 11,401 ft. (3,475 m) |
| Lowest Point: | Sea level |
| Area: | 29,762 sq. mi. (77,054 sq km) |

# DOMINICAN REPUBLIC

The Dominican Republic became independent from Spain in 1821, but was under Haitian rule from 1822 through 1844. The present republic was founded in 1844, also the year the present national flag was first raised. The flag was designed by Juan Pablo Duarte, the founder of the La Trinitaria movement, the revolutionary movement responsible for the Dominican Republic breaking away from Haiti and forming a separate country. The flag is still referred to as the Trinitaria flag.

The color red represents the spilled blood and the fire of hardships endured by the organizers of the state who fought to obtain and secure freedom for all. The white cross symbolizes the sacrifices of the people. The color blue stands for liberty.

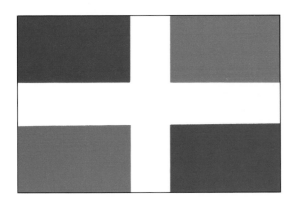

| DOMINICAN REPUBLIC | |
|---|---|
| Official Name: | Dominican Republic |
| Capital: | Santo Domingo |
| Languages: | Spanish |
| Religions: | Roman Catholic |
| Exports: | Sugar, nickel, coffee, tobacco |
| Imports: | Food, petroleum, raw materials, machinery |
| Highest Point: | 10,417 ft. (3,175 m) |
| Lowest Point: | -131 ft. (-40 m) |
| Area: | 18,704 sq. mi. (48,425 sq km) |

# HAITI

Haiti became independent from France in 1804 and is the second-oldest free nation in the Western Hemisphere, preceded only by the United States.

During their struggle for independence, Haitians used the French Tricolor; however, upon independence, General Dessalines deleted the white band and only used the blue and the red colors, despite the fact that other troops used flags of black and red. (The black symbolized the people's African heritage and the red represented other blood lines.) In 1805, a flag of vertical black and red panels was adopted; however, in 1807, Pétion resumed use of the blue-and-red flag, but in a horizontal arrangement. This flag was used until 1964, when President Duvalier readopted the black-and-red flag, which was flown until his fall in 1986; at that time, the blue-and-red flag was again restored.

The official Haitian flag has borne the arms on a white rectangle at its center since 1843.

| HAITI | |
|---|---|
| Official Name: | Republic of Haiti |
| Capital: | Port-au-Prince |
| Languages: | French |
| Religions: | Roman Catholic, Protestant, voodoo |
| Exports: | Coffee, bauxite |
| Imports: | Consumer goods, food, industrial equipment |
| Highest Point: | 8,773 ft. (2,674 m) |
| Lowest Point: | Sea level |
| Area: | 10,714 sq. mi. (27,739 sq km) |

# THE BAHAMAS

The Bahamas were for centuries a British colony, but in 1964 they obtained self-government. In 1973, they gained full independence, and the flag was designed the same year. The flag's elements are the result of a design competition. The color black represents the people of the Bahamas, while the gold and aquamarine symbolize the sands and the waters of the islands. It is said that the aquamarine color of the flag matches the color of the surrounding waters.

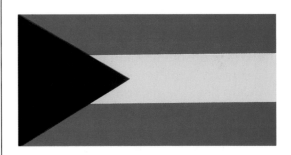

| BAHAMAS | |
|---|---|
| Official Name: | Commonwealth of the Bahamas |
| Capital: | Nassau |
| Languages: | English |
| Religions: | Baptist, Anglican, Roman Catholic |
| Exports: | Pharmaceuticals, rum, cement |
| Imports: | Food, manufactured goods, fuels |
| Highest Point: | 206 ft. (63 m) |
| Lowest Point: | Sea level |
| Area: | 5,382 sq. mi. (13,934 sq km) |

# CUBA

Cuba gained its independence from Spain in 1898 and from the United States in 1902. The "Lone Star" national flag of Cuba was designed in 1849 in New York City by Narciso Lopez, a leader of Cubans in exile who hoped to liberate their homeland from Spain. The Stars and Stripes of the United States was an inspiration for the design, but the three blue stripes represented its three departments, East, West, and Central. The star was suggested by a popular patriotic poem and symbolized the destiny of the island as an independent nation. The design of the flag was rendered by Miguel Terbe Tolon and sewn by his wife, Amelia. The flag was taken by a military expedition to Cuba in 1850, but it would be more than half a century until its adoption as the official Cuban flag. The red triangle symbolizes liberty, fraternity, and equality, as well as the blood sacrificed by Cuban patriots. Experts believe the triangle to be a Masonic symbol of equality.

*REPUBLIC OF CUBA (REVOLUTIONARY); UNOFFICIAL NATIONAL FLAG 1868-1869*

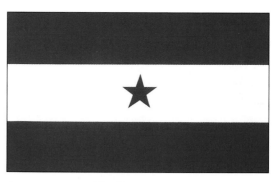

*CUBA; CIVIL ENSIGN C. 1899-1902*

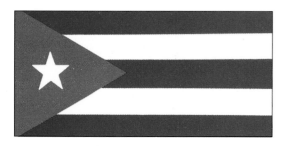

*LEFT: Cuban flags decorate a tobacco factory.*

© Randy Taylor/Leo de Wys, Inc.

| CUBA | |
|---|---|
| Official Name: | Republic of Cuba |
| Capital: | Havana |
| Languages: | Spanish |
| Religions: | Roman Catholic |
| Exports: | Sugar, nickel, shellfish, tobacco |
| Imports: | Capital equipment, raw materials, petroleum, food |
| Highest Point: | 6,476 ft. (1,974 m) |
| Lowest Point: | Sea level |
| Area: | 44,218 sq. mi. (114,480 sq km) |

*RIGHT: A view of Havana, Cuba's largest city and capital.*

© Richard Vogel

REPUBLIC OF CUBA; WAR FLAG 1934–1944

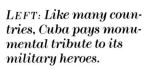

*RIGHT: Spanish architecture and forty-year-old American cars are common sights in Havana.*

*LEFT: Like many countries, Cuba pays monumental tribute to its military heroes.*

*LEFT: A palm tree is featured on the national coat of arms of Cuba.*

## JAMAICA

Jamaica gained independence from Britain in 1962 and adopted its national flag the same year. The colors in the flag have no obvious political significance, but represent the following: yellow, the sunlight and natural resources; black, the burdens shouldered by the people, which they are still enduring; and green, the country's agriculture and hope for the future.

| JAMAICA | |
|---|---|
| Official Name: | Jamaica |
| Capital: | Kingston |
| Languages: | English |
| Religions: | Anglican, Baptist, other Protestant, Catholic |
| Exports: | Alumina, bauxite, sugar, bananas |
| Imports: | Fuels, machinery, transportation equipment |
| Highest Point: | 7,402 ft. (2,256 m) |
| Lowest Point: | Sea level |
| Area: | 4,244 sq. mi. (10,988 sq km) |

*Montego Bay in Jamaica is well known to sun-seeking tourists.*

## BARBADOS

Barbados became independent of Britain in 1966 and that same year, adopted its present national flag. Prior to independence, Barbados used a flag that bore a badge with Britannia grasping her trident (the trident represents rule over the sea). The present flag, designed by Grantley W. Prescod, the winner of the 1966 flag competition, also uses the trident symbol. Now, however, according to Mr. Prescod, the trident, of which only the head can be seen, links Barbados with its past but under new conditions. The three prongs of the trident's head represent the three principles of democratic government: of, by, and for the people. The color blue symbolizes the sea and the sky; yellow represents the country's sandy beaches.

| BARBADOS | |
|---|---|
| Official Name: | Barbados |
| Capital: | Bridgetown |
| Languages: | English |
| Religions: | Anglican, Methodist, Roman Catholic |
| Exports: | Sugar and sugarcane products, clothing |
| Imports: | Food, machinery, consumer goods, fuels |
| Highest Point: | 1,115 ft. (340 m) |
| Lowest Point: | Sea level |
| Area: | 166 sq. mi. (430 sq km) |

# ANTIGUA AND BARBUDA

Antigua and Barbuda existed as an associated state of Britain from 1967 until independence in 1981. The national flag, designed by Reginald Samuel, was chosen from six hundred submissions and was adopted in 1967.

The sun in the flag represents the dawning of a new era and the red is said to represent the energy of the people. The blue, yellow, and white together symbolize Antigua's tourist interests, the sea, sun, and sand. The V shape stands for victory.

*Antigua, like other Caribbean islands, has many beautiful beaches.*

| ANTIGUA AND BARBUDA | |
|---|---|
| Official Name: | Antigua and Barbuda |
| Capital: | St. John's |
| Languages: | English |
| Religions: | Anglican |
| Exports: | Clothing, rum, lobsters |
| Imports: | Fuels, food, machinery |
| Highest Point: | 1,319 ft. (402 m) |
| Lowest Point: | Sea level |
| Area: | 170 sq. mi. (440 sq km) |

# GRENADA

Grenada was an associated state of Britain from 1967 until its independence in 1974. At that time, its flag was a horizontal tricolor of blue-yellow-green. In the center was an oval bearing a representation of a nutmeg, the chief export of the island. As a British colony, Grenada had displayed the Union Jack and the British Blue Ensign with a badge designed by British authorities. As in other countries gaining independence, the citizens of Grenada wanted a distinctive flag which would represent their national personality in a clear and striking fashion. At the time of independence in 1974, the present flag was adopted. At the hoist is a stylized nutmeg. The stars of the flag, in Afro-Caribbean colors, represent the seven districts of the island.

| GRENADA | |
|---|---|
| Official Name: | Grenada |
| Capital: | St. George's |
| Languages: | English |
| Religions: | Roman Catholic, Anglican, others |
| Exports: | Cocoa, nutmeg, bananas |
| Imports: | Food, machinery, construction materials |
| Highest Point: | 2,756 ft. (840 m) |
| Lowest Point: | Sea level |
| Area: | 133 sq. mi. (344 sq km) |

# CHAPTER EIGHT

# *South America*

The northern part of South America was ruled by Spain as New Granada (modern Venezuela, Colombia, Ecuador, and Panama) until the early 1800s. In 1819, the independent state of Gran Colombia (Greater Colombia) was formed and included the now-independent republics of Colombia, Ecuador, and Venezuela. Once separated, each of these countries pursued independence differently; however, their earlier alliance is echoed in the colors of their flags, all of which are derived from the tricolor, the symbol of their revolt against Spanish rule. The yellow, blue, and red tricolor was designed by Francisco de Miranda in 1806. He intended the colors to symbolize the "Spanish despots" (red) and the sea (blue) that lay between them and a free people (yellow). Miranda's liberation attempt of 1806 failed within the year; however, the tricolor was again taken up by Simón Bolívar, the Latin American champion of liberty, often called the "George Washington of Latin America."

It was Bolívar's dream that South America, after obtaining freedom from Spain, would form a federation of states. As an impetus, he founded the Federal Republic of Gran Colombia from the formerly mentioned territories. It is from this organization that the other interpretation of the South American tricolor originates, the "golden America which is separated by the blue sea from bloody Spain."

## *COLOMBIA*

Although independence from Spain was proclaimed by various provinces in Colombia as early as 1811, it was not until 1821 that freedom was secured by military success. The early flags showed the colors yellow, blue, and red in horizontal stripes with an emblem in the upper hoist corner. At first this was a very complicated coat of arms, but in 1817 blue stars for the united provinces were substituted. After 1819, there were three stars for the new state of Gran Colombia, consisting of New Granada (Colombia), Venezuela, and Quito (Ecuador). After the federation dissolved in 1829–1830, Gran Colombia created a new flag with equal vertical stripes of red-blue-yellow. In 1861 it reverted to the unequal horizontal stripes of yellow-blue-red. In both cases, naval vessels and merchant ships added special emblems in the center of the flag—either a coat or arms or a star.

| COLOMBIA | |
|---|---|
| Official Name: | Republic of Colombia |
| Capital: | Bogotá |
| Languages: | Spanish |
| Religions: | Roman Catholic |
| Exports: | Coffee, cotton, fuels, bananas |
| Imports: | Transportation equipment, machinery, metals, chemicals |
| Highest Point: | 19,029 ft. (5,800 m) |
| Lowest Point: | Sea level |
| Area: | 439,737 sq. mi. (1,138,479 sq km) |

## *VENEZUELA*

Venezuela became independent from Spain in 1811, but its national flag dates back to Miranda's failed liberation attempt in 1806. This version of the Miranda tricolor is the most original, with three equal stripes. The flag was first raised in 1811, with the liberation of New Granada. From 1822, when Venezuela joined with Ecuador and Colombia, until 1836, Venezuela used the same flag as Colombia (see **Colombia**). In 1859, Venezuela readopted the flag in its original form, adding the seven stars to represent the seven provinces of Venezuela that rebelled against Spain. Over the years, alterations have been made on the stars.

| VENEZUELA | |
|---|---|
| Official Name: | Republic of Venezuela |
| Capital: | Caracas |
| Languages: | Spanish |
| Religions: | Roman Catholic, Protestant |
| Exports: | Petroleum, iron ore |
| Imports: | Machinery, transportation equipment, manufactured goods |
| Highest Point: | 16,427 ft. (5,007 m) |
| Lowest Point: | Sea level |
| Area: | 352,144 sq. mi. (915,574 sq km) |

## *TRINIDAD AND TOBAGO*

In 1962, Trinidad and Tobago became independent from Britain and adopted a distinctive national flag of their own. Previously, they had used the British Blue Ensign with a shield in the center of the fly end. On land the Union Jack was the official government flag. The new design was developed in a very brief time because independence was announced at the end of May 1962, to take place at the end of August. This followed the breakup of the West Indies Federation of which Trinidad and Tobago had been a part. The new national flag was designed by a government commission. The colors represent the following: black, unity of purpose; red, warmth and vitality; and white, the sea and equality. The flag's colors are also said to represent the basic elements of earth, fire, and water, "which, according to the populace, encompass their past, present, and future; and inspire them as one united, vital, free, and dedicated people."

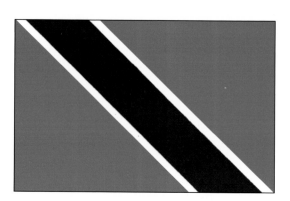

| TRINIDAD AND TOBAGO | |
|---|---|
| Official Name: | Republic of Trinidad and Tobago |
| Capital: | Port of Spain |
| Languages: | English |
| Religions: | Roman Catholic, Hindu, Protestant, Muslim |
| Exports: | Petroleum, ammonia, food |
| Imports: | Petroleum, machinery, transportation equipment |
| Highest Point: | 3,085 ft. (940 m) |
| Lowest Point: | Sea level |
| Area: | 1,980 sq. mi. (5,126 sq km) |

# GUYANA

Guyana became independent from Britain in May 1966 and adopted its national flag the same year. The flag was designed by Whitney Smith, director of the Flag Research Center in Massachusetts. The original design had a golden arrowhead on a red field with a green triangle at the hoist. The red and green were reversed and narrow stripes of white and black were added by the parliament of Guyana. Red, yellow, and green were chosen in part to reflect the African heritage of many Guyanese.

The symbolism of the colors is interpreted in the following manner: red is for the zeal and energy manifested by the people in their work of building their nation; yellow represents the country's mineral resources; black stands for the resoluteness that will hold together the nation in its progress; and white symbolizes the country's numerous rivers.

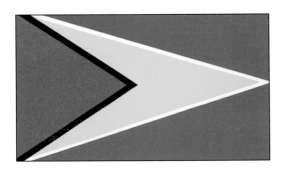

| | GUYANA |
|---|---|
| Official Name: | Cooperative Republic of Guyana |
| Capital: | Georgetown |
| Languages: | English |
| Religions: | Christian, Hindu, Muslim |
| Exports: | Bauxite, sugar, rice |
| Imports: | Manufactured goods, petroleum, food |
| Highest Point: | 9,094 ft. (2,772 m) |
| Lowest Point: | Sea level |
| Area: | 83,000 sq. mi. (214,887 sq km) |

# SURINAME

Suriname was occupied by the Netherlands from the eighteenth century until 1975. Before its independence, this nation's flag had a white field (representing peace) bearing an oval line linking five stars, each a different color (white, black, brown, yellow, and red) to symbolize the country's multiracial heritage.

The present flag (the result of a compilation of ideas submitted by the public) was adopted upon independence and combines the colors of the country's political parties: the green represents the National party; red, the Hindu *Vatan Hitkari;* and white, the People's party.

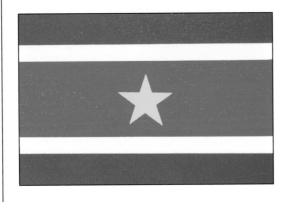

| | SURINAME |
|---|---|
| Official Name: | Republic of Suriname |
| Capital: | Paramaribo |
| Languages: | Dutch, English, Hindi, Sranang Tongo |
| Religions: | Hindu, Muslim, Roman Catholic, Moravian, others |
| Exports: | Alumina, bauxite, aluminum, wood and wood products |
| Imports: | Capital equipment, petroleum, iron, steel |
| Highest Point: | 3,749 ft. (1,143 m) |
| Lowest Point: | Sea level |
| Area: | 63,037 sq. mi. (163,203 sq km) |

# FRENCH GUIANA

French Guiana was once the site of the famous penal colony, Devil's Island, from 1938 until it was phased out in 1951. At the present time, French Guiana is a French department (state) and sends a single senator and deputy to the French Parliament. Guiana is administered by a prefect and has a Council General of sixteen elected members. Like other parts of France, French Guiana hoists the French Tricolor.

| | FRENCH GUIANA |
|---|---|
| Official Name: | Department of French Guiana |
| Capital: | Cayenne |
| Languages: | French |
| Religions: | Roman Catholic |
| Exports: | Shrimp, wood, rum |
| Imports: | Food, manufactured goods, petroleum |
| Highest Point: | 2,723 ft. (830 m) |
| Lowest Point: | Sea level |
| Area: | 35,135 sq. mi. (90,965 sq km) |

## ECUADOR

Ecuador, which means "Equator" in Spanish, first rose against Spain in 1809. The Miranda tricolor (see **Colombia** and **Venezuela**) was raised in Quito, the capital, in 1822, when Ecuador was finally liberated from Spain and became a part of Greater Colombia. Ecuador was a member of Greater Colombia until 1830, but continued to use the flag until 1845, when it reverted to a blue-and-white flag used by the freedom fighters of Guayaquil. In 1860, the Miranda tricolor was readopted; however, the country's arms were placed in the flag's center to distinguish it from the flag of modern Colombia. The flag's colors are interpreted in the following manner: yellow stands for the sunlight, the grain, and the country's natural resources; blue, the rivers, the sea, and the sky; and red, the blood of the patriots who fought for liberty and justice.

LEFT: *The iguana is only one of many unusual species living on the Galápagos Islands of Ecuador.*

© K. Benser/Leo de Wys. Inc.

|  | ECUADOR |
|---|---|
| Official Name: | Republic of Ecuador |
| Capital: | Quito |
| Languages: | Spanish, Quechua |
| Religions: | Roman Catholic |
| Exports: | Petroleum, bananas, coffee, cocoa, fish |
| Imports: | Machinery, raw materials, transportation equipment |
| Highest Point: | 20,702 ft. (6,310 m) |
| Lowest Point: | Sea level |
| Area: | 109,483 sq. mi. (283,451 sq km) |

## PERU

Peru gained its independence from Spain in 1821, but didn't adopt its present national flag until 1825. It is said that the inspiration for the flag's design originated during the 1820 war against Spain. Legend has it that General José de San Martín, leader of the Army of the Andes and liberator of Peru, saw a flight of birds with white crests and red wings and, interpreting the vision as a good omen, remarked, "See, the flag of liberty!"

The colors were combined in various forms until 1825, when the present flag's vertical form was established.

|  | PERU |
|---|---|
| Official Name: | Republic of Peru |
| Capital: | Lima |
| Languages: | Spanish, Quechua, Aymara |
| Religions: | Roman Catholic |
| Exports: | Copper, silver, petroleum, lead, zinc |
| Imports: | Machinery, transportation equipment, food, manufactured goods |
| Highest Point: | 22,205 ft. (6,768 m) |
| Lowest Point: | Sea level |
| Area: | 496,224 sq. mi. (1,284,724 sq km) |

*ABOVE: This statue honors the Inca leader Mancocapar.*

*LEFT: Machu Picchu, a tribute to the achievements of the ancient Inca empire in Peru.*

# BOLIVIA

In 1825, Upper Peru (actually the south-eastern part of the country) withdrew from the rest of the region and named itself the Bolivar Republic, after Simón Bolívar (see **Peru**) who was their first president. Later, the name was simplified to Bolivia. The country's first flag was red with green stripes at the top and bottom and five gold stars within wreaths. In 1826, the top stripe was made yellow. In 1851, the stripes were placed in their present order and made into equal widths. The flag's colors are interpreted as follows: red represents the country's fauna; yellow, its minerals; and green, its flora. The country's arms appear on the state flag.

| **BOLIVIA** | |
|---|---|
| Official Name: | Republic of Bolivia |
| Capital: | La Paz |
| Languages: | Spanish, Quechua, Aymara |
| Religions: | Roman Catholic |
| Exports: | Tin, natural gas, silver |
| Imports: | Machinery, consumer goods, fuels |
| Highest Point: | 22,579 ft. (6,882 m) |
| Lowest Point: | 325 ft. (99 m) |
| Area: | 464,164 sq. mi. (1,201,721 sq km) |

*A scarlet macaw from Bolivia.*

© Mike J. Howell/Envision

# BRAZIL

Brazil, unlike other Latin American nations, was colonized by Portugal, not Spain. Its flag origins are therefore tied to Portugal, an influence seen in the blue and white of the central globe, also the colors of the national flag of Portugal.

Brazil became independent from Portugal in 1822 and chose green and yellow as its new flag colors. Green represents Brazil's vast jungles, while yellow symbolizes its gold and other mineral resources. The diamond shape in the flag also represents Brazil's mineral resources.

During the revolution of 1889, the imperial coat of arms was removed from Brazil's flag and replaced with a celestial globe with a night sky of the Southern Hemisphere. The globe bears a scroll with these words, *Ordem e Progresso,* "Order and Progress." The twenty-three stars in the night sky represent the country's states and federal district, which contains Brazil's capital, Brasília, at the time the flag was most recently changed. Supposedly, the image of the sky is that of Rio de Janeiro the night the Brazilian empire was overthrown, on November 15, 1889.

| **BRAZIL** | |
|---|---|
| Official Name: | Federative Republic of Brazil |
| Capital: | Brasília |
| Languages: | Portuguese |
| Religions: | Roman Catholic, Protestant |
| Exports: | Soybeans, coffee, transportation equipment |
| Imports: | Petroleum, machinery, chemicals, pharmaceuticals |
| Highest Point: | 9,888 ft. (3,014 m) |
| Lowest Point: | Sea level |
| Area: | 3,265,075 sq. mi. (8,453,279 sq km) |

*OPPOSITE: Sugarloaf is an unusual geological formation in the bay at Rio de Janeiro.*

KINGDOM OF PORTUGAL, BRAZIL, AND ALGARVE;  STATE FLAG 1816–1822

EMPIRE OF BRAZIL; NATIONAL FLAG 1822–1889

# CHILE

Chile first sought independence in 1810 but didn't achieve it until 1818. The first flag of Chile, raised in 1812, was a blue, white, and yellow tricolor. In 1817, a new flag was adopted with red substituting for yellow. Later that same year, the present arrangement of the colors was adopted and the star was added; it was this flag that was flown during the final declaration of independence. (Until 1854, however, the flag without the star was used by civil vessels and private citizens.)

Two different officers of the Nationalist Army of Chile are responsible for the flag's design, Antonio Arcos and Charles Wood (a citizen of the United States serving as a volunteer officer of engineers), which is undoubtedly modeled after the United States' Stars and Stripes. The blue represents the Andean skies; white, the snows of the Andes; and red, the blood shed for freedom.

ABOVE: Beagle Channel in Patagonia, Chile.

BELOW: Magellanic penguins at the southernmost part of Chile, Punta Arenas.

| CHILE | |
|---|---|
| Official Name: | Republic of Chile |
| Capital: | Santiago |
| Languages: | Spanish |
| Religions: | Roman Catholic, Protestant |
| Exports: | Copper, molybdenum, iron ore, paper products |
| Imports: | Petroleum, sugar, wheat, capital equipment, motor vehicles |
| Highest Point: | 22,572 ft. (6,880 m) |
| Lowest Point: | Sea level |
| Area: | 292,135 sq. mi. (756,338 sq km) |

# ARGENTINA

Argentina was once, with Uruguay and Paraguay, a province of Spanish Vice-Royalty of the River Plate, or Rio de la Plata (the Silver River—later to be called the Argentine, from which Argentina derives its name). Argentinians first rose against Spanish rule in 1810, and after the Spanish viceroy was deposed, the people wore blue-and-white cockades. In 1812, General Belgrano adopted the triband flag for use with the Liberation Army soldiers. Later, after independence was declared in 1816, this flag was used as a civil ensign. In 1818, the state flag was created by placing the sun, called the Sun of May, in the flag's center. This flag is used today for civil purposes. The Sun of May symbol was originally adopted as a part of the arms in 1813 and was later used as a flag emblem by José de San Martín, who led the Army of the Andes.

| ARGENTINA | |
|---|---|
| Official Name: | Argentine Republic |
| Capital: | Buenos Aires |
| Languages: | Spanish |
| Religions: | Roman Catholic, Jewish, Protestant |
| Exports: | Meat, corn, wheat |
| Imports: | Machinery, lubricating oils, iron, steel |
| Highest Point: | 22,831 ft. (6,959 m) |
| Lowest Point: | -138 ft. (-42 m) |
| Area: | 1,068,301 sq. mi. (2,765,831 sq km) |

# PARAGUAY

Paraguay became independent from Spain in 1811, earlier than the other River Plate provinces (Argentina and Uruguay; see **Argentina**), and adopted its national flag in 1842. The flag was modeled after a flag dating back to 1812.

Paraguay uses the only double-sided national flag in the entire world. On the front side is the state emblem, which was adopted in 1842 but is said to have been in use since around the time the country became independent. The star is referred to as the "May Star," named for the liberation date of May 14, 1811. On the reverse side is the Treasury Seal, a lion sitting beneath a staff with the cap of Liberty on it and the motto: *Paz y Justicia* (Peace and Justice). The flag's colors were supposedly inspired by the French Tricolor.

| PARAGUAY | |
|---|---|
| Official Name: | Republic of Paraguay |
| Capital: | Asunción |
| Languages: | Spanish, Guarani |
| Religions: | Roman Catholic, Mennonite |
| Exports: | Cotton, soybeans, wood products |
| Imports: | Machinery, fuels, motor vehicles, food |
| Highest Point: | 2,625 ft. (800 m) |
| Lowest Point: | 151 ft. (46 m) |
| Area: | 157,048 sq. mi. (406,597 sq km) |

# URUGUAY

Uruguay, named for the Uruguay River, which flows through the country, was once a province (along with Paraguay and Argentina) of the Spanish Vice-Royalty of the River Plate (see **Argentina**). Uruguay's first separatist flag was that of José Artigas; it was hoisted in 1815 and is now the military flag. It consisted of three horizontal stripes of blue-white-blue with a red diagonal band from upper hoist to lower fly. Other flags of these colors were also used. Some versions of that flag unofficially bore the black inscription *Libertad o Muerte*, "Liberty or Death."

However, in 1828, when independence was won, the people decided to create a flag that did not resemble the flag of Argentina; and the United States' Stars and Stripes was chosen as a model. Uruguay originally adopted a flag that had nineteen stripes, although the flag now has nine. The nine stripes represent the nine departments (states) of the country. The sun in the canton is the Sun of May emblem (see **Argentina**).

| URUGUAY | |
|---|---|
| Official Name: | Republic East of the Uruguay |
| Capital: | Montevideo |
| Languages: | Spanish |
| Religions: | Roman Catholic, Protestant, Jewish |
| Exports: | Wool, hides, meat, textiles, transportation equipment |
| Imports: | Petroleum, machinery, transportation equipment |
| Highest Point: | 1,644 ft. (501 m) |
| Lowest Point: | Sea level |
| Area: | 68,037 sq. mi. (176,148 sq km) |

# CHAPTER NINE

# *Other Flags of Significance*

Flags are often used for other purposes than to denote allegiance to a nation, king, or state. Flags are often used to signify international causes.

Another international movement with a readily identifiable flag is the environmental organization Greenpeace, whose flag can be seen on land and at sea, near those who seek to protect the environment. The emblems of the dove, the olive branch, and the rainbow are all taken from a Bible story about the flood. The flag's green field represents not only the idea of conservation, but hope.

Organizations such as the Boy Scouts of America and the Girl Scouts also have their own flags, which signify their ideals of cooperation and service.

●

One of the oldest uses of flags is for signaling at sea. During war between the Greeks and the Persians (547–478 B.C.), signals were sent with flaglike objects, vexilloids, by both sides. During the Middle Ages, Venetian and Genoese fleets had more elaborate signals. The first known flag made specifically for signaling was the "Banner of the Council," introduced for the British fleet in 1369 and used to summon captains to an admiral's ship. Signals were also transmitted by raising ordinary flags in special codelike positions. The first regulated flag code signal system dates back to the 1600s in England. In the 1700s, numeral flags were invented; these could be combined to create messages. Each ship also had pennants to represent its name, and the numerals could be used to symbolize letters of the alphabet.

In 1812, Sir Home Popham introduced special flags for the letters of the alphabet, and by 1889, there was a single flag for each number and letter. On January 1, 1901, the first International Code of Signals was introduced.

Semaphore, a system of flag signaling that involves the changing of positions of the flags held in both hands to represent different letters and numbers, is also used on land.

During the United States Civil War, a signaling method was developed that utilized one flag with a white field and a blue horizontal center stripe to represent the dots and dashes of the International Morse Code.

●

Flags are also used in many sports, including team games, water sports, auto racing, golf, gymnastics, skiing, and cross-country events. In these cases, the flags are used as signals, as route markers, and to denote team allegiance, as is the case with baseball pennants.

Soccer linesmen use flags to indicate to the referee when the ball has gone out of play or when a player has broken the rules of the game. In soccer, flags are also used to mark the corners of the playing field.

The Olympic flag, which originated in 1913, has five rings that represent the five continents that take part in the games. The opening and closing of the games is signaled by the raising and the lowering of the Olympic standard. Each Olympic game has its own flag as well.

Flags are also used to signal the beginning and the end of events, such as in auto racing. In auto racing, the best-known flag is the checkered flag, which is used to end the race and to designate a winner. An auto race is often started by waving the host country's national flag, and many other flags are utilized as specific signals to the drivers, who need to identify what is occurring in an instant. When the victor crosses the finish line, the checkered flag is ceremoniously waved. After the winner passes, the end of the race is signaled to the runners-up by holding the flag motionless.

© Susanna Pashko/Envision

© Steve Brown/Leo de Wys, Inc.

© Ruth Sondak/FPG

*ABOVE: The display of many flags in this fashion is known as "dressing the ship."*

*ABOVE, RIGHT: The checkered flag is a familiar sight at automobile races.*

*RIGHT: The peace symbol seen during antiwar protests in the 1960s was derived from the semaphore letters 'N' and 'D', which stand for nuclear disarmament.*

*ABOVE: Originally the flag of the Council of Europe, the flag of the European Community was adopted in 1986.*

*ABOVE, RIGHT: The flag of the 1992 summer Olympic games.*

*RIGHT: The United Nations flag embodies some of humankind's highest aspirations.*

# *Appendices*

## *MAKING YOUR OWN FLAG*

Of course, the best way to enjoy a flag is to fly it! The following information will help you construct a flag that has the same design on both sides.

It is important to use the same type of fabric for the entire flag; if this is not possible, at least use material that is of similar weight and texture. Don't forget that both sides of the flag will be visible once it is hoisted. Use a heavy material that will be able to stand up to the weather. Some fabrics to look for include: cotton Dacron blends; permanent-press cotton home-spuns (kettlecloth); Mexican cottons; wool; and rayon.

If your flag is going to be used for outside service, there is a special material that is made to government flag-making specifications. This material is called bunting and it is fade- and weather-resistant. Bunting is a type of weave, previously made of wool. It is now available in cotton and artificial fabrics such as nylon and polyester. It comes in a wide variety of colors and can be bought by the bolt or by the yard from flag and banner companies.

If you cannot find bunting, test any of the previously mentioned fabrics for resistance to the weather and fading by the sun by leaving a sizable strip outdoors for several weeks. Then compare it to the original lot.

You will also need two grommets (metal eyelets that reinforce the holes in the fabric through which the rope used to raise and lower the flag is inserted; the grommets also prevent the rope from tearing the flag), ⅜ inch (1 cm) or larger, and a strip of white canvas material for your heading (hoist binding). Along this strip you can sign your name and the date and record a short message. If your flag will be exposed to severe weather, you may wish to sew small rectangles of material to each corner where your grommets will be attached to the canvas hoist to prevent tearing.

Decide what color of thread you wish to sew the entire flag with. It is best to use a running stitch or a quilting stitch. You can easily review these two stitches in any quilting book if you have questions.

**1)** Use a pattern for whatever design you choose so that your emblems (stripes, sun, moon, stars, etc.) are even and regular. Lay the pattern over your flag and carefully draw on the shape.
**2)** You can then sew these shapes on top of the drawings, but be careful not to over-stitch, as this can cause tearing in inclement weather.
**3)** Next, fold and press the canvas hoist piece into place, lengthwise, and remember to allow for the two grommets, each of which are to be placed into a hole about 1 inch (2.5 cm) from each end.
**4)** Take the top and bottom fly (the length of the flag) and fold them under about ½ inch (1 cm) and hem them into place. The hoist edges (the outsides) should be merely turned about 1 inch (2.5 cm) under and sewn with at least three rows of stitches to promote long wear.
**5)** Turn the edges of the heading so that they are even with each other, and line up the top and bottom edges with the flag. Now place the grommets into the holes and secure them.

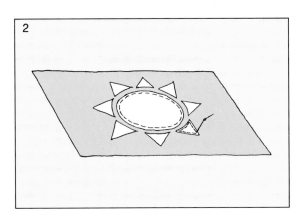

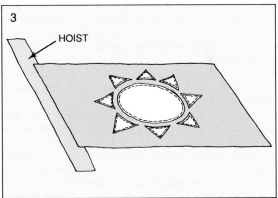

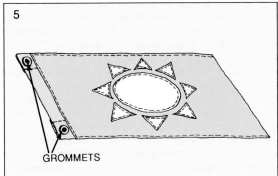

HOIST

TOP FLY

BOTTOM FLY

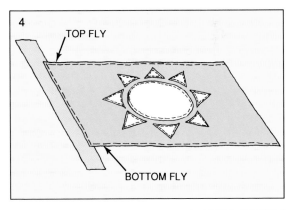

GROMMETS

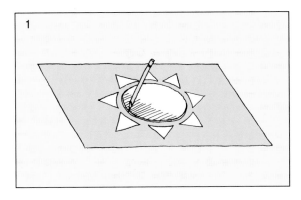

## *FOLDING A FLAG*

A flag which is to be stored for any length of time should be rolled or folded loosely so that it will not be damaged. If it is to be used again soon, it may be folded according to the protocol developed for folding the Stars and Stripes, as described below. In any event, a flag should not be rolled or folded if it is damp or soiled.

**1)** With a person holding each end, fold the flag lengthwise through its center, with the stripes at the top. Pull taut to remove any wrinkles.
**2)** Fold the flag again lengthwise, this time revealing the stars. Again, pull out to avoid wrinkles.
**3)** Beginning at the striped end, fold the corner to create a forty-five-degree triangular fold.
**4)** Continue working the triangular fold from one end to the other. Smooth and pull out wrinkles as they occur.
**5)** If possible, tuck the loose end of the fold into another fold in order to secure. Only the stars should be visible.

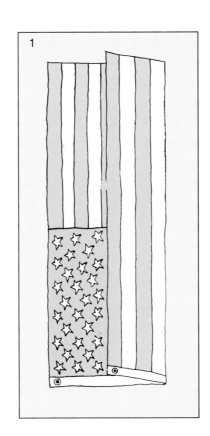

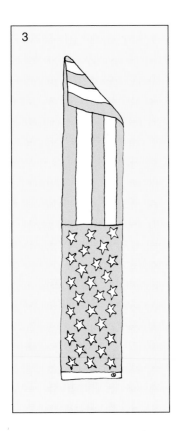

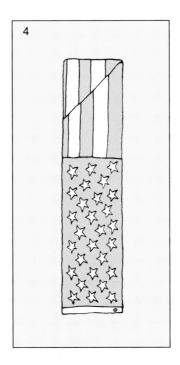

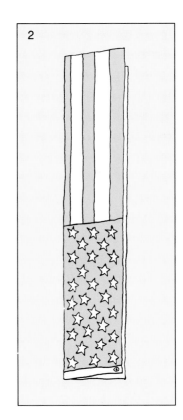

## CARING FOR YOUR FLAG

The quality of material and workmanship, the overall conditions of usage, the type and amount of area pollution, and proper care are the four factors that will impact a flag's life.

An indoor flag should be shaken often to dislodge dirt and dust. Pollutants such as cigarette smoke, airborne cooking grease, and furnace silt can settle into the flag's fabric, causing the colors to appear dingy and eventually breaking down its fibers.

Generally speaking, flags should be hand-washed. As soon as tears or frays appear, they should be mended, but use caution with stitching because overstitching can result in future damage. It is a good idea to occasionally check the flagpole or rod, since splintering and/or rust will not only promote damage to the flag from rips and frays, but will also allow oxides to eat through the flag's fabric.

It is important to remember that outdoor flags are extremely vulnerable to weather changes and air pollution caused by everything from exhaust fumes to acid rain. If the flag is exposed to moisture, allow it to dry completely before storing it. This will minimize mildew and fabric rot. If the flag's colors bleed during a heavy rain, wash the flag in warm water before hanging it up to dry.

Eventually, wear and tear will catch up with a flag, making reconstruction necessary. When this happens, take the flag apart piece by piece (separate the canton from the hoist and cut out any designs such as stars, stripes, etc.), and use the old flag as a pattern for a new one. This will lend a sense of continuity and will help you to repeat your original design.

## FLAGPOLES

Generally, flagpoles are available from flag or banner companies. If you must buy your flagpole elsewhere, carefully investigate the type of wood that it is made of, since many types of wood will splinter and rot. Wooden poles, while lending an authentic look, need constant upkeep to avoid chipping paint and rough edges that can tear the flag as it is blown about by the wind. The best solution is to purchase a steel flagpole from a flag company. This type requires almost no upkeep and can be installed into the earth, concrete, or onto the side of a building, and can weather strong winds.

## FURTHER READING

Admiralty of Great Britain. *Drawings of the Flags of All Nations.* London: H. M. Stationery Office, 1989.

Baraclough, E. M. C., and William Crampton. *Flags of the World.* Rev. ed. London: F. Warne, 1981.

Crampton, William. *The Complete Guide to Flags.* New York: Gallery Books, 1989.

Elting, Mary, and Franklin Folsom. *Flags of All Nations and the People Who Live Under Them.* In consultation with The Flag Research Center and Edwin M. Moser. New York: Grosset & Dunlop, 1969.

Evans, I. O. *The Observer's Book of Flags.* London: F. Warne, 1975.

Neubecker, Ottfried. *A Guide to Heraldry.* New York: McGraw-Hill, 1979.

Ortegal, Adelaide. *Banners and Such.* New York: Resource Publishers, 1983.

Pedersen, Christian. *The International Flag Book.* New York: William Morrow, 1971.

Smith, Whitney, and The Flag Research Center. *Bibliography of Flags of Foreign Nations.* Boston: G. K. Hall, 1965.

Smith, Whitney. *Flags Through the Ages and Across the World.* New York: McGraw-Hill, 1975.

## RESOURCES

There are thousands of vexillologists (those who study flags), vexillophilists (flag collectors), and vexillographers (flag designers) around the world. The first flag magazine was published in 1961, followed by the first conference (1965) and organization (1966) for those interested in the subject. New members, both amateurs and professionals, are welcome to participate in the vexillological organizations that have grown up around the world. They can help the hobbyist locate exhibits to visit, flags and flag publications to buy or trade, activities to participate in, and similar resources. Every two years there is an International Congress of Vexillology open to all interested participants. For more information, contact one or more of the following:

**THE FLAG RESEARCH CENTER**
Dr. Whitney Smith, Director
Box 580
Winchester, Massachusetts 01890

Founded in 1961; publishes the bimonthly *Flag Bulletin*

**CANADIAN FLAG ASSOCIATION**
Mr. Kevin Harrington
50 Heathfield Drive
Scarborough, Ontario
M1M 3B1

Founded in 1985; publishes the quarterly *Flagscan*

**FLAG SOCIETY OF AUSTRALIA**
Mr. Ralph Bartlett
Box 142
Collins Street Post Office
Melbourne, Victoria
3000 Australia

Founded in 1983; publishes the quarterly *Crux Australis*

**THE FLAG INSTITUTE**
Mr. Michael A. Faul
44 Middleton Road
Acomb, York
Y02 3AS United Kingdom

Founded in 1971; publishes the biannual *Flagmaster*

# GLOSSARY

**Armorial banner**: The design of a coat of arms made up as a flag

**Badge**: A distinctive emblem that can be added to a flag or used alone

**Banner**: (a) An armorial banner; (b) a flag suspended from a crossbar or between two poles; (c) a flag of intricate composition

**Bicolor**: A two-colored flag

**Border**: A wide band of color surrounding a field of a different color

**Bunting**: A lightweight, loosely woven fabric used for flag material; cloth in flag colors used for decoration

**Canton**: The upper hoist quarter of a flag

**Charge**: An emblem or device added to a flag or shield

**Civil flag and ensign**: The version of the national flag used by private citizens on land (civil flag) and sea (civil ensign)

**Cockade**: An ornament (rosette) or other significant colors worn as a badge

**Courtesy flag**: The civil ensign of a host country flown by a foreign vessel

**Crest**: The upper portion of a coat of arms, resting on the helmet

**Cross**: A normal cross has two arms at right angles that extend to the edge of the flag or shield

**Couped cross**: One whose arms do not extend to the edges of a flag or shield

**Disk**: A single-colored circular area

**Emblem**: Any badge, device, or distinct symbol

**Ensign**: The flag flown at the stern of a boat to indicate nationality, or by government departments on land; includes air usage as well

**Field**: The background color of a flag or shield

**Fimbriation**: A thin band of color that separates two other colors

**Fly**: The half of a flag away from the flagstaff

**Gonfalon**: An elaborate flag, usually of intricate design, hung from a crossbar

**Hoist**: The half of a flag nearest the staff; to raise a flag

**Inglefield clips**: Quick-release clips that are used to secure a flag to the halyards

**Jack**: A flag flown at the bow of a ship to indicate its nationality

**Jolly Roger**: Common name for flag supposedly used by pirates

**Length**: A flag's horizontal dimension

**Livery colors**: The main colors of the field and main figure on a coat of arms

**Merchant flag**: See **Civil flag**

**Mon**: The stylized emblem characteristic of Japanese heraldry

**National flag**: The flag used by a recognized nation-state; it may have several forms: civil, government, military

**Naval ensign**: The form of the national flag that naval vessels use

**Obverse**: The side of a flag seen when the staff is on the spectator's left

**Pennant**: A small, often tapering, flag

**Prize flag**: The flag used to indicate a winner in a yachting competition

**Reverse**: The side of the flag seen when the staff is on the spectator's right

**Saltire**: A diagonal cross

**Scandinavian cross**: A cross with unequal horizontal arms

**Staff**: The pole from which a flag is flown

**Standard**: (a) A vexilloid; (b) a large gonfalon; (c) a heraldic flag in livery colors with badges; (d) common name for heraldic banner; (e) ceremonial flag of a mounted military corps; (f) flag of a head of state

**State ensign and flag**: Versions of the national flag used for official purposes by the government at sea (ensign) and on land (flag)

**Streamer**: A very long, narrow flag

**Swallowtail**: The fly end of a flag from which a triangular portion has been cut; used often in Scandinavian countries

**Triband**: A flag of only two colors divided into three, generally equal areas

**Tricolor**: A flag of three different colors, often in equally divided sections

**Vexillology**: The scientific study of flags

**Vexilloid**: An object carried on a pole that realizes many of the functions of a flag

**Vexillum**: A Roman standard consisting of a cloth hung from a horizontal bar attached to a pole

**Width**: The vertical dimension of a flag

# INDEX